Preservation and Conservation of Library Resources

Preservation and Conservation of Library Resources

Dr. P. Balasubramanian
M.A., M.B.A., M.C.A., M.L.I.Sc., M.Phil., PGDPR, Ph.D.
University Librarian & Head
Department of Library & Information Science
Manonmaiam Sundaranar University
Tirunelveli 627012
Tamil Nadu
India

Ess Ess Publications
New Delhi

Preservation and Conservation of Library Resources

ISBN : 978-93-87698-36-9
Price : 825/-

First Published 2021

Published by:
Ess Ess Publications
4831/24, Ansari Road,
Darya Ganj,
New Delhi-110 002.
INDIA
Phones: 23260807, 41563444
Fax: 41563334
E-mail: info@essessreference.com
www.essessreference.com

Cover Design by *Patch Creative Unit*

Printed and bound in India

Dedicated to
MY BELOVED PARENTS

Contents

Preface

As Knowledge has become multi-dimensional, multidisciplinary it became a fast growing part in information revolution. In this "TITLE" book, main objective is to get knowledge about preserving resources of Libraries

Inside this book we have discussed about concept, methods and implication regarding Library Resource Management. Subject that matter is discussed with Basic English so that the readers can get better understanding.

I gave my complete effort to make it valuable, useful and enrich it with my views so that it give complete sense and benefit to readers. I hope who goes through it will find it interesting and worth reading. All constructive feedback is cordially invited.

Suggestion to new ideas for further improvement of this book shall be greatly appreciated and acknowledged.

I acknowledge my heartfelt gratitude to Prof. Dr. A Rangasamy for invaluable advice and suggestions.

Finally, I would like to acknowledge the pleasure of working with publishing team of Ess Ess Publications, New Delhi.

— **Dr. P. Balasubramanian**

Acknowledgements

The author feels extremely indebted to Dr. K. Pitchumani, Hon'ble Vice-Chancellor, Manonmaniam Sundaranar University, Tirunelveli. We also thank Dr. S. Santhosh Baboo, Registrar, Manonmaniam Sundaranar University, Tirunelveli and all the teaching and non-teaching staff members of the M.S. University, for giving us constant encouragement for writing this book.

We would be a benefit killer if we do not acknowledge the services of Ess Ess Publications, New Delhi for their efforts in bringing out this book in a record time. Suggestions for further improvement of the book are most welcome.

— Dr. P. Balasubramanian

1

Concept of Preservation and Conservation

LEARNING OBJECTIVES

After reading this unit, you will be able to

- Explain the concepts, need and history of preservation and conservation.
- Evolution of Writing Materials.
- Inherent characteristics of the Library Materials like Manuscripts, Books, Periodicals and Newspapers.

Introduction

Conservation of library material is most difficult issue in the present librarianship. Libraries are more focused on scattering of data than the safeguarding of library materials. Methods for sorting out and distributing data are growing quick, however the preservation aspect is as yet being disregarded. In the event that due consideration isn't given for the preservation of library material, at that point there is all the probability that our social legacy and "country's aggregate" memory may vanish. Our libraries are without organised experts in protection. In this specific circumstance, E. W. Sautéing says," Libraries have requested and library schools have prepared assistants in book assortment, in classifying, and arrangement however not in protection and conservation. The terms, 'preservation', conservation and recovery have been utilized conversely in library writing until most recent years.

At present conservation is the more explicit term and is especially utilized in connection, to explicit items, though 'preservation' is a more extensive idea covering conservation just as activities identifying with guarding, upkeep and recovery of library assortments. Christopher Clarkson accentuates this more extensive viewpoint when he expresses that 'preservation' includes each aspect of library life, it is as he says, preventive medicine. The burden of everybody who strolls into, or works in, a library for Clarkson conservation is 'the specific procedure of making safe, or in a specific way usable, delicate period objects' and retrieval communicates rather broad rebuilding and substitution by current materials inside a period object, providing food for fate of progressively strong use. He perfectly recognizes the three terms by relating them to the degree of tasks connected to an item; recovery infers real modifications, conservation negligible and preservation none. Another British writer, Diana Grimwood Jones brings up a further valuable peculiarity among preservation and conservation, the previous term is principally alarmed about guaranteeing that the first ancient rarity is kept up and secure, though the last structure applies to different procedures for safeguarding the scholarly content.

1.1. PRESERVATION AND CONSERVATION: CONCEPT, NEED & HISTORY

Conservation is a term, which grasps three firmly related thoughts, "preservation, security and maintenance." According to American Council of Learned Societies (ACLS) territory of preservation initiates with the formation of content, reaches out to publication further to acquisition and after that available storage in the library for access and use. This implies preservation alarms with writers, distributers, bookkeepers and readers. Be that as it may, library administrators have greater duty of saving the library reading materials. The term conservation is two folded, for example preservation and reclamation. In preservation, additive measures are taken to stop or to check or retard deterioration, and in rebuilding, extraordinary treatment is to be given to the reading materials so as to take them back to their unique true shape. Rebuilding is a specialized region and requires extraordinary abilities, which may not be feasible for every bookkeeper to have it. The library material is taken care of either by the library staff or the clients.

The terms preservation, and conservation are considered by different associations. International federation of Library Associations and Institutions (IFLA) has characterized these terms as under.

Preservation : Includes all the administrative and money related thought including storage and convenience arrangements, staffing levels, strategies, systems and techniques engaged with safeguarding library and document materials and the data contained in them.

Conservation : Denotes those particular arrangements and practices associated with guarding library and documented materials from depreciation, harm and rot, including the strategies and systems conceived by specialized staff.

Harrods' Librarians Glossary has characterized these terms as :

Conservation (Archives) : The utilization of synthetic substances and other physical methods in treatment or storage to guarantee the preservation of a record.

Preservation (Archives) :

(i) The essential elements of an archive vault to give sufficient facilities to the consideration, security and maintenance of the archives of whatever sort,

(ii) Specific individual and aggregate measures taken for the fix, reclamation, assurance and support of the archives.

Preservation is a more general term than conservation and is an administration procedure; conservation is a specialized and/or art process. Conservation implies the safeguard and perceptive utilization of our usual assets. Conservation means guarding these assets so the more noteworthy number of individuals may utilize them insightfully.

J. R. Wit makes reference to that regular assets are constrained, yet additionally a large number of them can likewise be effectively harmed or decimated. Men chop down trees and dig out metals for use in structures and production. They obliterate timberlands to clear the land for cultivating. They contaminate streams and make the water unfit for use. They exhaust the dirt and make it futile for developing more harvests. Conservation is concerned with the assets we need today, yet in addition with assets for what's to come. In every age, each a lot of the world decreases in light of the fact that our populace is developing quickly. Conservation likewise denotes, defending Human Resources. Our prosperity depends not just on soil, trees, and minerals. It likewise relies upon our wellbeing and on the administrations we get. Conservation of human and characteristic assets helps make and keep our homes, our nation, and soil and all God's creations better places in which we live.

1.1.1. Preservation and Conservation History

In making the library the biggest and most complicated universal library in the globe, one of the early librarians of Congress was aware that restricted funds had to not hinder its route of procurement from a decent facility to meet the requirements of U.S. legislators. Several fresh methods have been used in order to transfer big amounts of free material to the library. In the wake of collections development, questions emerged as to whether holdings were maintained properly. Space was not only an issue, but collection care was also taken.

Although the library has a tradition of minimizing imprint decay and enhancing processes and treatments, it has only been organizationally central to its operations since 1967. In 1965, the Library and the Association of Research Libraries held a national preservation planning meeting jointly sponsored by the Library to re-examine its conservation operations and to assess the need for science values and sound management in the program. In light of this development, the Library has now established its conservation operations in order to protect the collections and enhance their helpful lives as a result of the global reaction to the catastrophic inundation which took place in Florence in 1966. Components of the preservation directorate–the office of the conservation director (including the MAD) plus 4 divisions: the Binding and Collections Care division, the Conservation Division, the Preservation Research and Testing Division and the Preservation Reformatting Division are currently implementing a coordinated program.

Institutional Growing Pains : Congress founded the Library in 1800 when it moved from Philadelphia to the new capital of Washington. The 24 April act establishing the Library was to allocate five thousand dollars' to buy books which could be required for congressional use,' to house books in an "appropriate apartment" at the Capitol, and to monitor the buyout, furnish the catalog and "devise and lay down" the Library regulations. The book was a joint committee of the Congress. The new organization took a strong interest of Thomas Jefferson in specific. Initially, the Congress Library (LC) was a library for use by Congressional members and the Supreme Court's judges only. The first Librarian of the Congress purchased some 3,000 volumes in its first dozen years for this tiny constituency, covering a wide array of subjects.

The Congressional reference library was replaced by a single trade, following the British burning the Capitol building during the War of 1812 and the later loss of original library collections, when the Congress authorized Thomas Jefferson to buy the entire 6487-volume multilingual library in 1814 for $23,940. It included quantities of all architecture, geography and science. Before Jefferson argued that his collection would appear too broad for Congress, "no topic that could not be referred to by a member of Congress."4 Collections grew slowly, as did the amount of individuals who had access to the library, but the Library was still essentially used by lawmakers, the diplomatic corps, and senior citizens. Then, the library's holdings were destroyed by a significant fire on Christmas Eve 1851.

Meehan (librarian) wrote to Maryland Senator Pearce, Chairman of the Joint Committee on Library: "This morning, at about half past seven o'clock, a fire was set in the main room of the Library of Congress and almost all the fire was destroyed before the fire was subdued," he said. A joint resolution authorizing an investigation into the origin of the fire was assumed two days later by the House of Representatives. Three days after Capitol Thomas U Walter's incident Architect revealed that defective chimney flu was causing the fire. Funds were earmarked to replace the lost books and build a fresh facility for library alone.

Ainswürd Rand Spofford's arrival as a Congress bibliothecar in 1864 marked a fresh era in the Library's fulfillment of its mandate as a legislative resource center. Spofford seized upon registration of copyright as an excellent chance for extending the library's collections at no price to his library. It would not prevent him from bringing "variety of books and river of data" into the shops. His efforts to lobby paid off in 1870. The legislation was amended to require any copyright party to submit two copies in any of the books, maps, diagrams, dramas or music, graving, cutting and printing, or photographs. The Library obtained 371,636 books, 257,153 magazines, 289,617 pieces in music, 73,817 images, 95,249 printed papers and 48,048 maps in the first 25 years following this revision. And over the years this free material flow has remained unabated.

Spofford has also influenced a statute that has given the Library many copies of the Congressional Record and the Large U.S. Statutes free of charge. He spoke about these issues in an exchange program with foreign governments which at the moment had diplomatic relations. Consequently, the Library has the world's biggest and most comprehensive publications collection. In addition, Spofford has paid attention to traditional techniques of purchasing materials through donations from collectors and buyers in relation to these innovative approaches for extending the Library's stock and access.

All accessible space was used quickly, as could be anticipated. The scenario had reached crisis dimensions in the mid-1870s. Shelving hasn't been performed ordinarily anymore. The construction, which began in 1886 and ended in 1897, of a separate building for the library (now called the Jefferson Building) solved the physical problem of housing collections for approximately 35 years and provided for the first time to the general public reading rooms and research areas and expositions. The Annex built in the 1930s provided extra storage and work space when the material quantity was once again larger than the space at hand. "The Annex" was built in 1930.

A 1960s Congressional directive to obtain "all library products of worldwide worth" led in a growing number of annual receipts for the Library of Congress, to the extent that now more than 2.5 million articles are published each year. The construction of another building again addressed the physical difficulties caused by the growing amount and the higher amount of employees involved in processing and serving income receipts.

The third structure - the Madison Building was occupied in 1980. It houses the Law Library and many of the Library's management and staff operations, including the Librarian's Office, the Congressional Research Service, and the Copyright Office. In addition to the Preservation Directorate, components of the Office of the Associate Librarian for Library Services that are housed here are the Acquisitions Directorate, the Cataloging Directorate, and some of the custodial divisions of the Public Service Collections Directorate, including the Manuscript Division; the Prints and Photographs Division; the Motion Picture,

Broadcasting and Recorded Sound Division; and the Music Division.

Although a growing number of library materials is properly housed, the issue was obviously focused on maintaining these resources. The 119 million items of the Library include 18,000,000 books, 2 million photos, 12 million photos, 4 million maps and 53,000 manuscripts, covering 500,000 kilometers, including study documents in more than 450 languages and almost every medium of preservation and communication of information and creativity. The vast amount of holdings together with the huge variety of formats and materials and the uniqueness of many of their products make it especially exciting and extremely difficult to deal with the conservation of the Library of Congress.

The conservation of the library of Congress has been recorded since the early 1800s. But policies and programs have been formalized only in latest times. The Preservation Directorate, using adequate treatments and techniques, today seeks to maintain a extensive track record of American history and creativity and a universal collection of human information for the present and future uses of Congress and the nation.

The Directorate had an average staff of 172, the budget of an appropriated $11 million in the final year of the 20th century, as well as the program, or budget, to maintain all library holdings including the approximately 10,000 articles, which are added each working day to the institution's collections. The Annual Report of the Congress librarian from 1898 indicates that one of the first concerns LC expressed about preservation was when John Russell Young said of "the questionable quality of the paper so many of the library's materials are printed on." The paper which was then made in mass of pulp was far less permanent than the paper produced before the 1940s, which used rag. When Yung decried the use by publishers of this inexpensive, unstoppable document, many works coming to the library threatened to collapse into a waste heap without record value in a few years.

The paper quality was not only the Library's continuous problem but also the impact of Washington, D.C. Area on the holdings of the library. Herbert Putnam, Young Successor as Librarian of the Congress, took one of the initial measures to minimize environmental deterioration in the early 1900s. Learning that sunlight deteriorated leather bindings, Putnam had developed a scheme to control sunlight in rooms by learning British studies. He directed the building superintendent to design a "system of blinds that safeguard the western windows" of the stack regions that are usually flooded by sunlight.

The "Report of the Committee of the Leather Arts for Bookbinding" confirmed the opinion that bookbinding leather was then used inferior to that of the previous 50 years; mechanical causes (changes in manufacturing and tanning techniques) were also attributable to the degradation, and also "to the damaging impact of light and fumes, which in many libraries was prevalent then."

Interestingly, Michael Faraday revealed to the Royal Institution some 60 years previous comparable results from one of the earliest inquiries into the causes and prevention of leather breakdown. This was the result of the request made by the Athenaeum Club to decide what caused their books and leather chairs to deteriorate. "The harm to heat and sulfur fumes from light gas then used was outlined by Faraday."

Washington was waiting a few decades later on to develop appropriate air conditioning and humidification technologies, to deal with the oppressive warm and humid summer climate in Washington. The climate of the Library is now controlled to preserve temperature and moisture conditions suitable for distinct collection kinds. In all three LC buildings systems for filtering off contaminants have also been mounted.

1.1.2. Centralization and Modernization of Preservation Activities

In 1965, a joint meeting between the library congress and the Association of research libraries focused on the need for a national preservation program, prompted the library to reassess how well it met LC's demands and how it was able to take the lead in library conservation operations in the United States and elsewhere. The Library further acknowledged "the need for a more efficient conservation program to apply science principles and sound techniques of administration."

In these occurrences in the 1960s, the Library became more and more conscious that the conservation operations were fragmented and badly coordinated. In order to preserve its wide collection for future generations, better administrative control, a centralized budget and more science strategy were necessary. Plans to centralize most conservation work into one office were therefore developed.

In this manner, it would be possible to adopt a more coordinated and effective strategy to conservation issues and better uses resources. The plans also included the establishment of an extended conservation program for the conduct of research and testing and a modern conservation center under direct control of the library.

Consequently, in 1967 the Library took a fresh conservation strategy by centralizing all conservation operations in one department under one administrative body and the required resources to promote these operations. On 15 May that year, an assistant director was established to preserve the collections, and the name of the preservation office in the administration was changed to the preservation office. This new unit was entrusted with the overall management of the conservation programs of the Library.

The operation led by Frazer G. Poolle led to the

creation, with the support of the Processing services and the collection maintenance function (the transfer was transferred from the Stock and Reader Division), of an preserving microfilming section, a research and testing laboratory, and a restoration group. In 1968 an agreement was reached on the transfer from the Government Printing Office to the Library of command over basic issues such as staff and creation of technical norms, as well as processing and equipment specification for preserving the Library Collections.

Mr. Poole was succeeded by Norman Shaffer as Assistant Director for Preservation in 1978. That year the Preservation Office was transferred to Research Services. The preservation administrator's title was changed from Assistant Director to Director for Preservation when Dr. Peter Sparks was appointed to that position in the Preservation Office in 1981.

1.1.3. The Preservation Directorate Today

Overview : The conservation program is run by the conservation director, who is in charge of all the operations of the conservation directors, coordinating them and guiding them. The Director reports to the Librarian's Associate Librarian, who reports to the Congress Librarian. The Directorate coordinates and oversees all Library operations related to the conservation of library material and its physical security.

The Directorate is active in the development and implementation of instant and long-term library conservation projects with other domestic and foreign study institutions and organizations, Plan and coordinate library employees and employers ' education conservation and data programs to increase awareness about conservation, It offers reference and data services and emergency reaction and retrieval aid in matters of preservation, conservation of and physical custodianship and library material, including the material of vandalism and theft or damaged by fire, flood, or other catastrophes and technical liaison and offers help to other libraries, external agencies, institutions or people.

Mission : The Conservation Directorate of the Library is the world's biggest conservation and preservation facility. It is America's biggest and most ancient operation, the biggest conservation lab and was the first to include a part of materials science studies and testing. The Directorate of Preservation's mission is to ensure long-term, initial or reformatted access to the intellectual material of the library's collections. The task is achieved directly by providing conservation, tying up and repair, accommodation, reformatting, research and advancement on materials and preservation science, and employees and user training, and indirectly by coordinating and supervising all library-wide work on the preservation and physical safety of library materials.

Range of Activities and Collections : In order to maintain their collections, and make them more available for customers, the Library of the Congress employs the complete variety of traditional techniques of conserve-binding, new techniques such as paper deciding and the digitization of initial materials. These interventions include keeping materials in the right setting; ready for emergency situations like water drainage; ensuring that the collection is properly taken care of and managed by both employees and scientists; stabilizing fragile and rare materials in alkaline buffered or pH-neutral containers so that they can degrade and extend their helpful life considerably.

Management of conservation programs presents many difficulties at the Library of Congress. The library collections are wide and diverse, and many are the iconography of our nations ' struggles and victories for more than two hundred years. The contents of President Abraham Lincoln's pockets on the night of his assassination, the drawing of a macaroni machine by President Thomas Jefferson, the National Association for the Development of Colored People (NAACP) Corporate records, pictures of immigrant workers during the Grand Dépressions, television epics are not presented in any other library. The collections include leather, fleece, palm leaves, papyrus, paper, nitrates, CD-ROM, wax cylinders, vinyl records and magnetic tape. They also come in a number of different formats.

Outreach Programs : The Preservation Directorate has a powerful domestic and global program of outreach and offers the congress, public organizations, other libraries, organizations, and the general public with data on conservation. The Office played an important part in the organization and hosts both domestic and international conservation planning meetings for US organizations. As stated below, the Conservation Division of the Directorate administers an active internship program through which staff from around the globe receives sophisticated training in specific conservation abilities.

1.1.4. Conservation Division

The Library of Congress was the first library in the United States to create a conservatory office (initially known as the Restaurant Office). Intrinsically precious manuscripts, prints, drawings, photos, maps, rare books that must be maintained in the initial format, the Division of Conservation is accountable for examining, documenting, processing and preventive care. This job needs the expertise of the conservatives in book, paper, collection and photography, who develop unique skills through academic and internship training. Conservatives treat (stabilize and restore), rare and unique collections in specially equipped labs to minimize further deterioration. Conservators advise the custodian divisions on the handling of book material in relation to therapy.

No professional conservative staff development took place overnight. Since the start of the 1900s the initial

GPO restaurateur (known as Bindery Workers) had carried out traditional restoration operations. In the early 1960s, Frazer Poole persuaded the management of the Library that the approach to conservation management and exercise should be professionalized. After he had trouble recruiting a US citizen who had been eligible to head the new restructuring office, he got approval to attempt to employ a laboratory manager from other nations and other seasoned conservatives.

In 1969, Poole recruited and worked closely with England to plan the growth and staffing of the new office for two years. In 1971, Waters moved to Warsaw to become the full-time restore officer of the library. On the advice of Waters, Fraser Poole employed two other British conservators who also played a critical role when the program was initially developed: Donald Etherington, who was a ten years trainer at his office in 1970, and Chris Clarkson, who headed the Rare Book Conservation Section for five years. Due to their professional participation and catastrophe regeneration experience after the 1966 Florence Flood as well as their book preservation training experience under the Roger Powell and the two famous English book conservators, Poole employed this team of conservation executives.

1.1.5. Conservation and Preservation Method

According to Ross preservation can be achieved by two methods, one is preserving the artifact, and the other is preserving the intellectual contents.

1.1.5.1. Preserving The Artifact (Physical)

(i) Refurbishing and collection maintenance

(ii) Fumigation

(iii) Protective enclosures.

   (a) Encapsulation

   (b) Phase (Phased) boxes

(c) Other Boxes.
(d) Document folders
(e) Slipcases
(f) Shrink-wrapping

(iv) Binding
(a) Recessing
(b) Sewing through the fold
(c) Double-fan adhesive Binding
(d) Over sewing
(e) Other binding methods
(f) Strengthening paperbacks.

1.1.5.2. Preserving The Intellectual Content

Reformatting

(a) Photocopying
(b) Microfilming
(c) Photography [Film]
(d) Digitization

Carolyn Horton has described the procedure for refurbishing the collection. According to her following steps are necessary:

(a) Set up a work area and obtain equipment and supplies.
(b) Establish do cementation procedures.
(c) Remove the books from the shelves.
(d) Dust the books.
(e) Sort the books into two categories

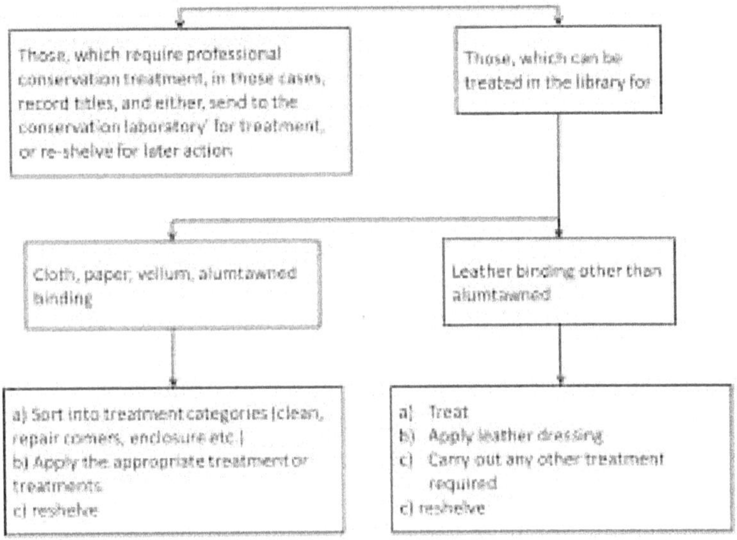

Fig. 2

The following conservation and preservation methods are normally used in the libraries.

1.1.5.3. Fumigation

There are a many synthetic substances which are fickle for example they dissipate, either in typical room temperature or with slight ascent in the equivalent. As the vapour of whatever unstable synthetic compounds are harmful to the insects, fungi, and so forth, those can be utilized for assurance against foes of the library accumulations. This strategy is known as fumigation. Vaporous chemicals used to clear out insects and so on are called fumigants. The synthetic compounds, which are typically utilized for this design, are either fluid or strong in ordinary condition. In those libraries where the issues of parasites and insects assault are moderate to high, or where there is sufficient plausibility of such issues, fumigation will demonstrate to be a very viable measure.

There are two kinds of fumigation, which are referenced by Mukhopadhya, one is customary and the other is vacuum fumigation. Vacuum fumigation is perceived as best method and for this framework a unique kind of steel fumigation chamber is needed. By and large, these chambers have a limit of 10 cu. Meter. Inside the chamber, books which are to be disinfected are kept either on book trolley or on racks. The entryway of the chamber-which is hermetically sealed, is bolted appropriately and air from the chamber is siphoned out. Subsequent to expelling the air around 4-5 kgs of ethoxide gas is presented with the assistance of electric siphon. Ethoxide gas is set up by blending 1 section ethylene oxide with 9 parts of carbon dioxide. This gas can obliterate all the parasites and bugs in an exceptionally brief period and can enter in all pieces of the books/archives effectively.

Another critical factor of this work is that it demolishes not just growths and grown-up insects but likewise spores and eggs, this office isn't accessible in most fumigation works. The ethoxide gas does not have any antagonistic impact on library accumulation. This framework requires around three hours to finishing the fumigation.

Thymol has been generally utilized in the past to disinfect infested library materials, in spite of the fact that its utilization is presently not allowed in the United Kingdom. It is done by setting up the affected materials in a sealed shut chamber with a dish of thymol crystal stones, which is then heated by being put close to a low wattage light. The material being disinfected is presented to thymol vapour for timings of shifting from three days to one week. The thymol vapour must not be breathed in and care must be taken to stay away from this, particularly when opening the thymol chamber toward the finishing of the treatment. Skin contact with the thymol crystals should likewise be stayed away from.

Ortho-phenyl phenol has been generally utilized in spite of certain questions about its viability as a fungicide. It very well may be used in a few different ways, for instance, by blending it with spirit and applying it as a tog or spray or by blending it with alchol and enabling it to vanish in a fixed chamber or other encased space. Likewise with thymol, care must be taken to abstain from breathing in the vapour of ortho-phenyl phenol or enabling skin to come into contact with it.

Tissue paper can be covered or soaked with a fungicide and put inside books, which should be dealt with; the book with its tissues is then put in tightened plastic sack for months. Chemical controls, for example, fumigation, and the use of pesticides and fungicides, generally offer just short term solutions for the issues they are expected to control for instance, when a chemical spray is used, just the form which is available is killed, and a little while later new mould spores will float in and start to develop if the conditions are favourable. Additionally fumigation in an encased chamber has no lingering mold control impacts, despite the fact that it should eliminate the mould effectively developing on the things treated. Parker ventures to such an extreme as to express that a significant part of the fumigation that is done in libraries isn't justified and positive expert approach is required to apply chemical control techniques, there can be medical hazards related with their utilization, and enactment carefully restricting the utilization of one-common synthetic drugs has been limited lately. Consequently it is in all respects emphatically suggested that master precautions should be looked for before any fumigation or other use of synthetic control measure is completed. It must be repeated that untrained staff which incorporates all library administrators – should not endeavour to apply any toxic substance fumigation strategies without first looking for master guidelines.

1.1.5.4. Encapsulation

Ross Harvey has depicted encapsulation as one of the preservation techniques. Single sheet thing can be exemplified between sheets of an artificially inert transparent plastic, for example, Mylar. Encapsulation is generally utilized for delicate things or where repeated usage is normal. Things encased as such can be taken care of and can without much of a stretch be expelled from the embodiment should this be required. Two Mylar sheets at any rate 2.5 centimeter bigger than the thing to be encapsulated are cut, the thing is laid on one sheet and the other put on the top, and edges of the Mylar are put together. Sealing should be possible either by utilizing two sided sticky tape, by sewing or by a progressively costly procedure, utilizing a ultrasonic welder. Around eight minutes for each thing is the time required for this method.

1.1.5.5. Lamination

This procedure includes hot-moulding a de-acidified archive with cellulose acetic acid derivation film of 23 microns (0.00088 inch) thickness and tissue paper in either a steam-heated level bed hydro-powered press or an electrically heated roller press. A sand-witch or envelope is set up by collecting the materials in the accompanying request.

Tissue paper cellulose acetate
film document
cellulose acetate film tissue
paper

Fig. 3

The de-acidified records of the volume are set so that there is a hole of 5vm in the middle of the sheets 1 and 8, 2 and 7, 3 and 6, 4 and 5 separately of an area. The course of action of the sheets is in step arrangement in the way appeared in the accompanying figure.

After lamination, this gap partition (laminated tissue)

winds up sufficiently able to fill the need of 'protect' for sewing the records into document covers to tie into a volume; the laminated protective layer can be solidified by putting in a slip of either bond paper or muslin fabric. During the planning of a sand-witch or envelope of matched records as depicted over every free section and the edges of the archives ought to be deliberately affixed to the acetic acid derivation film in their legitimate spots with a cotton swab or a craftsman's brush plunged in $CH_3)2CO$. Each sand-witch or envelope is then put between two sheets of 'Taffon' (tetrafluorethylene), engineered tar covered glass texture) before nourishing it into the press. On account of water powered (level bed) overlay, the sand-witch is secured with treated steel plates and a twofold thickness of blotting surfaces before being put on the platen. This is to ingest any disparities, which may exist on the outside of the platen or in the sand-witch, and to guarantee uniform weight on the material to be overlay, paying little respect to any distinctions in thickness at the edges of the report. At least one sand-witches might be put on one platen. In the last case, the request for the different materials on every platen is as per the following.

Stainless - steel plate
Blotters
Taflon
Sandwitch or envelope
Taflon
Blotter
Taflon
Sandwitch or envelope
Taflon
Blotter
Stainless – Steel Plate

Fig. 4

For acceptable and uniform cover, close to two sand-witches or envelopes ought to be put on every platen. Based on research completed in 1954-57, the United States National Bureau of norms has in certainty suggested that two sand-witches or envelopes be set on one platen.

The temperature required for overlaying paper records changes from 140-150°C and the weight from 22-36 kg/cm^2 relying upon the condition and sort of paper Between more than two and three minutes are for the most part required for cover, and the whole procedure, for example of warming and cooling, takes from seven to ten minutes. The cellulose acetic acid derivation, in view of the high weight, infiltrates the pores of the report paper just as the tissue paper.

Steam at a weight of 5.5 kg/cm2 is passed into the platens. Accordingly, the temperature ascends to the required 150°C inside two minutes. All the while, weight is connected to the platens. Following three minutes, the departure valve is opened and going water through them cools the platens. The required weight is kept up all through this activity. At the point when the platens have cooled, the weight is discharged and the covered records are evacuated. Yash Pal Kathapalia specifies certain safety measures which are essential when fixing records by this procedure. Care ought to be taken to guarantee that,

(a) There is no smoking in the room and that no stripped fire whatever is permitted; and

(b) There is appropriate air dissemination and that acetic acid derivation vapour are evacuated by methods for fumes fans.

During the last a quarter century, critical advances have been made in the field of reclamation a few ends have obviously developed.

(a) Film of polyvinyl chloride ought not to be utilized for the overlay of profitable archives.

(b) Overlay with cellulose acetic acid derivation film is a sheltered strategy for re-establishing archives.

(c) Polyethylene film utilized for overlay purposes can be delaminated, and is preferred for cover purposes over cellulose acetic acid derivation films.

1.1.5.6. Binding as A Preservation Measure

Restricting has been the major conventional preservation action in libraries. The particular storage of ties is to secure the book while being used or while it is being put away. In numerous libraries restricting is the main strategy used to save library material. Libraries tie materials for a few reasons, which are portrayed by Ross [30], which are as per the following

(a) To fortify things which are made in inadmissible arrangement for the harsh and tumble library use for example soft cover releases.

(b) Need to rebind things whose ties have turned out to be too worn to even think about offering security to the content of the book.

(c) To assemble in an all the more advantageously racked unit things which were issued sequentially, or which were issued independently for example leaflets.

(d) Security is another motivation to tie issues, as it is viewed as progressively hard to take an enormous bound volume than a little unbound thing.

(e) Binding is utilized a preservation device for delicate things, which expands their life as helpful things in library accumulation.

It is essential to take note of the various purposes behind restricting volumes in libraries and the subsequent necessities for ties of different sorts. In open libraries, restricting is utilized to accomplish the most extreme number of issues in a flowing gathering before a volume is disposed of; while restricting a volume in an examination library is to accomplish the greatest life workable for Several various types of ties in like manner use, these are as re-packaging, sewing through the overlay, Double-fan glue official, over-sewing and so forth. Business fasteners do most restricting work in the present libraries. Business library binderies have gotten unfavourable analysis in preservation circles since they have been seen to apply negligently one style of official to all material, paying little heed to how suitable the coupling may be.

1.1.5.7. Photocopying

Photocopying is best used to duplicate smaller things. It is a particularly reasonable format for intensely utilized things, where microfilm is hard to utilize and client obstruction Photocopying isn't suitable for works with hued or amazing highly contrasting delineations.

Photocopying has a few points of interest over different arrangements. It can, whenever required, produce a duplicate, which is in the equivalent or fundamentally the same as organization as the first. The outcome is moderately lasting if suitable soluble paper is utilized.

This procedure has a few detriments - One is the difficulty of the procedure, which may harm delicate things. Photocopying machines themselves are another reason for deterioration. Harm results from exposure to light, including ultraviolet light, unwanted heat, and from wrong structure, which powers materials into distressing positions. Paul Banks remarks that 'photocopying is a prime case of the two-edged sword.' The simplicity of protecting scholarly substance of library materials, and yet forcing significant weight on the material. Ties endure the greater part of the harm brought about by photocopying. Spine harm comes about because of pushing down on the authoritative to compel the pages level with the goal that content close to the inward edge can be duplicated. Flipping the book over the machine for duplicating successive pages can cause harm. Once in a while paper is being twisted or collapsed in-attentively or intentionally so far as that is concerned. Enormous bound volumes are especially in danger, and for sure numerous libraries don't permit them to be photocopied.

The British Library has been energetic as of late in creating and making accessible new printers and new strategies for duplicating. Three of these have been advanced the overhead copier, the picture digitizer, and electro luminescent replicating. The expense of these scanners are high; in 1985 the overhead printer was £ 6900 and the picture digitizer £ at least 20,000 Equipment required for the electro luminescent duplicating procedure cost about £ 200. As of late discharged scanners have observed preservation requirements for instance, the Xerox 5042, has a platen the finish of which is calculated at 35 degrees to permit better duplicating of internal edges without requiring power on the spine and has a discretionary foot-switch which permits two hands free for progressively cautious treatment of the materials.

1.1.5.8. Microfilming

There is no uncertainty that microfilming is right now the most generally utilized setup for duplicating the preservation. Real libraries all through the world are emphatically dedicated to microfilming. Microfilming has a long history of utilization in libraries and extensive sum is thought about it, including its life span whenever put away under fitting conditions. Microforms are delivered in a few arrangements, of these microform and microfiche are the well on the way to be experienced in libraries, albeit different organizations, similar to opening cards.

Libraries have habitually created or acquired 35 mm microfilm this size is best for the preservation purposes and it permits bigger size pictures with higher quality. Three sorts of microfilms are accessible; silver-gelatine, diazo, vesicular. Just silver-gelatine film which has been deliberately prepared to the proper guidelines ought to be utilized for archival original negatives which will be held for significant lots of time. Be that as it may, it is significant, that it ought to be watchfully put away and dealt with, as it is powerless to harm from parasites, water and mechanical scraped spot. Working duplicates can be done using silver-gelatin, however diazo and vesicular have points of interest where strength in everyday use could really compare to documented life. Both diazo and vesicular film is more affordable and more scratch safe than silver-gelatin. Most would agree that microfilming has cost favourable circumstances over other reformatting forms in current use and over reclamation medicines, particularly for things with numerous pages. Another real preferred position seen by Alan Calmes is the long haul solidness of microforms. On the off chance that they are made utilizing proper preparing measures, stockpiling conditions and taking care of methodology are watched, lifetime of over 1000 years have been communicated in the writing. The space-sparing component, particularly for serials is additionally huge.

Microforms can be inexpensively and effectively replicated once an original has been delivered. Paper duplicates of part or whole can be promptly created if microfilm or microfiche reader-printer are given. The gear expected to get to microforms is a simple optical gadget. It isn't 'cutting edge' with a high likelihood of getting to be out of date in a brief timeframe, similar to the instance of CD-ROMs and magnetic tapes. There are a few impediments to microfilm and its utilization. The hardware isn't easy to use and numerous readers have grumbled about headache, spinal pain and neck-injury. The regularly referred to contention against microfilming is that they are hard to utilize. A. J. Anderson has referenced the response of one reader about the utilization of microfilm.

"Be that as it may, these shocking microfilm users!

I had expected to appreciate a lovely day with the delicate pop of old papers in my grasp. Rather I had the fiend of a period pressing buttons, twinkling handles, and peering into an indefinitely lit screen. What a disaster it was! Also, what a crashing ache in the temples and the back of the neck I created before the entire unnatural experience was finished."

The generation, stockpiling and treatment of microforms require strict adherence to models, which can now and again be costly and hard to keep up. Thoughtless dealing with and storage can undoubtedly harm them. Be that as it may, as contrast with other preservation strategies, microfilming has been demonstrated as a best choice to protect library material for ages. Many microfilming activities have demonstrated that microfilm can be utilized for a long time with no harm whenever dealt with appropriately and put away in fitting atmosphere.

1.1.5.9. Preservation Photography

Preservation photography is one of the preservation techniques which is typically used uniquely to unique highly contrasting photographic prints. As indicated by Ross the point is to deliver an ace negative in addition to another negative (the break ace negative) from which prints can be taken as required. The ace negative ought to be put away in the most ideal condition for instance in low temperature stockpiling with the proper relative moistness, light and different levels, and should possibly should be gotten to on the uncommon events when the between time ace is exhausted and another interval Is ace is required. Prints can be taken from the master negatives at whatever point required, for instance to make a reference duplicate, or for display purposes. Top notch hardware and materials ought to be utilized and the administrations of expert photographers ought to in a perfectly contract.

1.1.5.10. Digitization

Libraries connect the past and the future, and preservation has consistently been a key role. Libraries guarantee that any sort of data is saved and made accessible for later use. Regardless of its extremely short history, digitization has an unfathomable awful record with regards to preservation. Witten and Brain Bridge referenced that

- Enormous measure of advanced data are as of now lost for eternity.
- Information innovations become out of date all around rapidly.
- Document and media organizations keep on multiplying.
- Technology measures won't tackle major issues in the preservation of advanced data.

This illustrates digitization as a preservation apparatus. In 1996, the US Commission on Preservation and Access issued the last report of a Task Force on the Archiving of Digital Information. An amazing gathering of 21 specialists had gone through a year in considering the issue. The end was disturbing that there is; at present no real way to ensure the preservation of advanced data. It is imperative to specify the endeavours of Yale and Cornell University. Project Open Book of Yale University was a multifaceted, multiphase innovative work venture. Its motivation was to investigate the possibility of enormous scale transformation of preservation microfilm to advanced symbolism by demonstrating the procedure in an in house research centre. The venture unfurled in a grouping of stages structured to some degree to enable the task to advance as the computerized imaging commercial centre changed. Yale changed over 2000 volumes from microfilm (speaking to 440000 pictures) recorded the volumes, put away the outcomes and tried a model web got to apparatus created by Xerox Corporation. Cornell University's venture

(Digital to Microfilm Conversion) was the attainability of embracing computerized innovation for preservation purposes. The over multi year exhibition task tried and assessed the utilization of high goals bitonal imaging to deliver PC yield microfilm (COM) that could fulfil national preservation guidelines for quality and lastingness. Over the span of the venture, 1,270 volumes and going with targets (speaking to 450,000 pictures) were filtered and recorded onto 177 reels of film. The undertaking lead to an evaluation of value, procedure and cost and to the improvement of proposals for the creation and investigation of preservation quality microfilm delivered from computerized imagery.

Research Libraries Group (RLG) started an agreeable microfilming task subsidized by NEH (National Endowment for Humanities) in 1986. These activities advanced wide acknowledgment of a meaning of preservation as lengthening out the life of data in reports, as opposed to the archives themselves when the records couldn't be saved in their original forms. NEH has considered microfilm the favoured preservation choice for embrittled distributed materials and an acknowledged access choice. Various prior tasks bolstered by Commission on Preservation and Access concentrated on digitization for preservation just as access. Inspite of expectations that microfilm could be supplanted by advanced imaging, early clients of this innovation come to welcome that basically digitizing material did not ensure its constant preservation. Because of this microfilm remains the favoured preservation reformatting system even as computerized imagery has accepted a noticeable job in upgrading access to such materials.

1.2. EVOLUTION OF WRITING MATERIALS

The invention of writing denoted a noteworthy achievement in man's social development. Starting with this achievement numerous cultures started to develop from carefully oral conventions to composed ones. Since the art of writing was found, about each type of composing material has been utilized. What pursues is a short recorded rundown of the more regularly utilized materials from stone to paper.

1.2.1. Stone

Stone was principally used for writing on lasting monuments and open structures. The writing on stone as a rule requires the usage of sledge and chisel. Since the vast majority are right handed given there would be an inclination to write the letters from right to left. Thus it is fascinating to take note of that we discover the progression of antiquated dialects, for example, Hebrew and Arabic to keep running from right to left. Stone is perhaps the most historical type of writing material.

Fig. 5

1.2.2. Metal

Fig. 6

Since not many sheets of metal with composing on them have ever been discovered it is assumed that metal was hardly used often for composing. Bronze tablets and copper sheets were utilized to give semi-perpetual quality and could be put away more effectively than rock. Archaeologists have found bronze tablets from old Roman archives that contain insights regarding negotiations and declarations.

1.2.3. Wood

Wood was utilized for short term purposes and very few such tablets have made through time, as the atmosphere in many nations isn't helpful for their preservation.

Fig. 7

1.2.4. Wax

An incredibly transitory strategy for writing was to scratch letters onto wax tablets. These were meager wooden boards secured with a fine covering of beeswax. The sheets could have little openings toward one side that allowed a ring to be put through enabling numerous sheets to make a flip book. The Latin name for this was codex and has turned out to be normal in alluding to any gathering of bound pages.

Fig. 8

1.2.5. Ostraca

Ostraca are broken shreds of earthenware that have inscriptions scratched onto them. Sherds were a decent wellspring of composing material since they were available in abundance and simple to utilize.

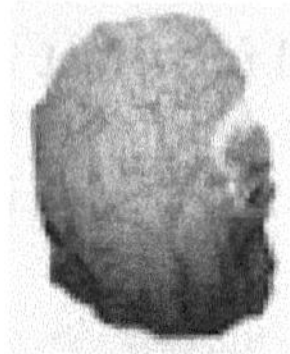

Fig. 9

1.2.6. Clay Tablets

Mud tablets are presumably the innovation of the Sumerians of southern Babylonia. The utilization of delicate mud tablets was mainstream until the Christian Era. Utilization of clay tablets wound up far reaching and was the general methods for composed communication all through Mesopotamia and the whole antiquated East.

The message to be sent was first written while the mud was delicate utilizing a dainty, sharpened apparatus to record the letters. This tablet was then heated to solidify it and make the message lasting.

Fig. 10

1.2.7. Papyrus

Papyrus is the 'grandfather' of paper. The thick reeds of the papyrus plant were stripped and after that cut into thin strips. These strips were spread out on panels in befuddle weaving pattern and tenderly beaten with a wooden hammer. The outcome, after drying, was a solid, leveled composing surface that could be winded up. Not only was it a flexible writing material it was likewise light in weight.

For storage they were wounded to make scrolls. For putting into practice purposes a long roll was a bit poorly arranged. To be read, a scroll must be unrolled as it was used. Due to this clumsiness, scroll length wound up regulated.

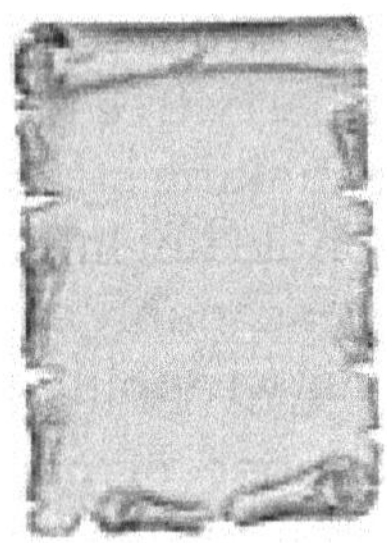

Fig. 11

1.2.8. Parchment

The main opponent of Egyptian papyri as a writing material was a surface produced using animal skins known as parchment. Composing on animal skins was known to be far reaching in the Assyrian time period.

Material is usually leather. Skins are washed, soaked, cleaned of hair and epidermis watchfully smoothed out. For parchment, the skins are not tanned but rather dressed with alum and tidied off with fine chalk. The more slender pelts of goats and sheep are ideally utilized for material over the thicker covers up of bulls. Young creatures delivered the best material and this is regularly called as vellum.

The dating of the Hebrew original inscriptions on parchment found at Muraba'at, close to the Dead Sea, was derived as to be around 750 BC. Parchment material seems to have turned into the typical writing material from this time on for lasting records while regulatory issues were as yet recorded on papyrus.

Fig. 12

1.2.9. Paper

Credit for the development of paper is commonly given to the Chinese over 2000 years prior. From the beginning, the Chinese utilized the hemp plant or the inward bark of the mulberry tree for fibre. Afterward, they found that great papermaking strands could be gotten by beating clothes, rope, or old angling nets into a pulp. Early Chinese paper was unreasonably coarse to inscribe a hard copy. They utilized it for wrapping and clothing.

The Chinese practise of papermaking spread to different parts of the world after a few Chinese papermakers were caught by Arabs. The paper business was built up in Baghdad in A.D. 795. Papermaking spread to Europe because of the Crusades and the Moorish invasion of northern Africa and Spain. The foremost paper plant in America was set up close Philadelphia in 1690.

In 1798, a Frenchman named Nicholas Louis Robert created a machine to make paper in continuous rolls as opposed to sheets. The Fourdrinier brothers, who were English traders, financed upgrades in this machine in 1803. The first American Fourdrinier machine was worked in 1827.

Fig. 13

The stone ground wood strategy for making wood pulp was created in Germany in 1840. In 1854, the first synthetically delivered wood pulp was made in England. During the 1850's chemists found that the strands in wood could be isolated by treating them with sulphurous acid.

In 1883, a German creator named Carl Dahl found that adding sodium sulfate to the soda procedure delivered a solid pulp. This revelation delivered the Kraft procedure. (Kraft implies quality in German). During the early 1900's, the Kraft procedure turned into the most significant pulping process, and the Fourdrinier machine turned into the essential gadget for making paper. It is fascinating to take note of that the Fourdrinier siblings did not get any royalties for their machine because of a patent error. (Smith, 1881)

Huge enhancements in papermaking since the mid 1900's incorporate thermo-mechanical pulping, engineered wires and felts, twin-wire machines, and the utilization of computer systems to control pulping and papermaking activities.

Today paper is the foundation of communication all through the world. Every year in excess of 300,000,000 tons of paper is created around the world. The normal North American buys more than 300 kilograms of paper a year. Americans read more than 350 million magazines, 2 billion books, and 25 billion newspapers per year - all imprinted on paper. More than 90 billion bits of trash mail are gotten yearly in the United States alone. (Asset Conservation Alliance, 2008). Our young ones play with paper dolls, paper veils, paper board games, and paper kites. When you go out to see a film the ticket you get is made out of paper, as are the holders and carrying plate for your popcorn and beverages.

On account of Computer systems, which were once expected to make our own a paperless society, we currently produce significantly more paper than any time in recent memory. Our cash, checks, stock endorsements, deeds of proprietorship, birth declarations and marriage licenses, exceedingly significant records which oversee our lives, are made out of paper.

1.3. INHERENT CHARACTERISTICS OF THE LIBRARY MATERIALS - MANUSCRIPTS, BOOKS, PERIODICALS AND NEWSPAPERS

Today the libraries are confronted with a wide range of kinds of material other than books. Original copies, maps, photographic material, various media material, microfilms, films and number of different things present the cutting edge library administrator new issues. These issues extend from procurement of these materials to the board and usage of it. Despite the fact that there are various regulations and standards for the handling of such materials, and in spite of the fact that these are relatable in a wide range of distinct and general libraries, in any case the genuine structure and content of inventory and index entries and the strategies for recording are liable to the work which they are proposed to perform. Truth be told, if these were possible to brief speculations regarding the variables administering the storage of extraordinary materials, following focuses would likely demonstrate highest in the minds of most custodians, availability, assurance, recording, economy away. The scientist has thought about after sorts of materials for digitization. To moderate and safeguard it, one should know its basic properties and remarkable highlights. These highlights would be useful while undertaking its digitization.

1.3.1. Manuscripts

Paul Mosher makes reference to that written by hand manuscripts were the main records of mankind's history for around 5000 years, until when printing ended up general all through the 'western World'. Manuscripts are valuable piece of our social legacy. Extraordinary old researchers committed their lives for making composed records of learning. Original copy is a term utilized for any report composed by hand or by a machine, for example, a or a PC. The word is frequently used to recognize a creator's unique adaptation of a work from the printed duplicate. Likewise, manuscript alludes to any transcribed record from old occasions until the presentation of imprinting during the 1400s.

Harrod's Librarians Glossary characterizes original copies as, "A report of numerous sorts which is composed by hand, or the content of a music or artistic structure in written by hand or typescript structure, and which, in that structure, has not been duplicated in different duplicates.

The oxford English Dictionary (another English word reference on authentic standards (1978) gives following importance of the term original copy

(a) Written by hand and not printed, curtailed as MS-singular and MSS-flural.

(b) A book, report or the like composed by hand, composing hand, composing of any sort as recognized from printed matter.

(c) Written character or composed report as a rule, composing instead of print

Papyrus manuscripts were first composed in Egypt right around 6000 years prior. The old Egyptians arranged the writing material from a reed like plant, called the papyrus. The original copy sheets were glued together into rolls or volumes, which were typically twenty to thirty feet long. The University of Michigan has almost 7,000 papyrus original copies, which is biggest in the U.S.A.

The utilization of skins as composing material is likely as old as the development of writing. Parchment was first utilized as manuscript material since it was less expensive than papyrus. It was moreover simpler to write on with a pen and it endured longer than papyrus. The priests of the medieval times duplicated onto parchment numerous old works of art from rotting papyrus rolls.

Paper was a development of Chinese, despite the fact that the word paper originates from the Egyptian papyrus. The old Chinese composed their most punctual manuscripts on thin wood or bamboo strips, or on silk rolls. After they figured out how to make paper, they looked for strategies for making it simpler to deal with.

1.3.2. Books

To characterize 'a book' is exceptionally troublesome. As indicated by David clement "A book which is hard to discover in the nation where it is looked for should be called simply rare; a book which is hard to discover in any nation might be called exceptionally rare, a book of which there are just fifty to sixty duplicates existing, or which shows up so sometimes as to propose that there never had been more, whenever than that number of duplicates, positions as incredibly rare; and when the entire number of duplicates don't surpass ten, this establishes intemperate rarity or rarity in the most noteworthy order" Mr. Burton don't concur with the order made by forebearing David about uncommon books. He expressed, "Books might be rare enough in the genuine or specific sense of the term, yet on the off chance that they are not so in the normal or abstract sense by being looked for after, rarity goes to no end. A volume might be exceptional, any stand very alone on the planet yet whether it is in this way, or one of a various family is never known, for nobody has ever wanted to have it."

Cunha has recognized after elements whereupon one can acknowledge which is the Book

- Relation to each tampered book to the whole accumulation.
- Research or chronicled significance of the volume
- Importance based on repeated usage.
- Permanent versus brief significance of each book.

Book collection varies from the general library

gathering in various ways

- Materials are remarkable and in this manner not agreeable to typical suspicions about condition or significance.
- Collections are bound to be created and kept up to adjust to some extract idea of greatness or fulfilment instead of to react to the prompt needs of any electorate.
- Frequency of utilization can't be thought to be dependable pointer of the estimation of an uncommon book to the gathering.
- Relatively little size and moderately mind-boggling value per things may allow a mindful ness to detail impractical in the enormous gathering.

Uncommon records have some inherent qualities. These records have implicit segment of learning Digitization has two features; one is quantitative while other is subjective. With regards to quantitative aspect, one needs to look towards record absolutely from the specialized perspective, for example, nature of that archive, how old it is and in what structure it tends to be changed. At what level it very well may be saved for example authoritative, cover, digitization, microfilming and so forth. Caroline Arms appropriately specifies that record does not simply mean something is written previously and which is required for conservation for the future, yet in that report, most noteworthy everlasting qualities humanities, most prominent fortune of learning is additionally contained in so as to make accessible and get to know this snippet of data, to the ages to come it is to be safeguarded. So here abstract component, the subjective component exists which is required for up-degree, upliftment and amazing quality of humankind for instance.

1.3.3. Graphic Material

Webster characterizes graphics as the craftsmanship or study of drawing-particularly mechanical drawing. As connected to visual materials, be that as it may, the term 'graphics' or 'graphics materials' has a more extensive significance than drawing alone. The first Greek graphikos included painting just as drawing and the action word 'graphein' signifies to compose just as to speak to by methods for lines. The idea of graphics can be depicted as materials, which convey actualities and thoughts obviously and coercively through a blend of drawings, words and pictures. The instructional qualities graphic materials lie for the most part in their ability to stand out and to pass on specific kind of data promptly. The graphic material can be sorted into following gatherings:

(a) charts

(b) diagrams

(c) graphs and

(d) notices

(a) Charts : Charts might be characterized as blends of graphic and pictorial media intended for the precise and legitimate imagining of connections between key certainties or thought. Charts can be named, tree chart, flow chart, tabular chart.

(b) Diagram : A diagram is an improved drawing intended to demonstrate interrelationships principally by methods for lines and images. While charts are exceptionally consolidated visual synopses of realities and thoughts, diagrams are considerably denser and depend intensely on representative methods for speaking to thoughts.

(c) Graphs : Graphs might be characterized as visual portrayals of numerical information. A table of figures may contain an abundance of significant data, yet a graph of similar information introduces the substance of that data rapidly and adequately. Besides, graph uncover significant connections in the information relationship, for example, patterns and varieties from typical. There are numerous sorts of graphs. Among those most normally utilized are the line, bar, circle or 'pie' and the pictorial graph. Each sort has certain points of interest.

(d) Notices : Written or formal information, notification, or warning about a fact, required to be made in law or imparted by an operation of law. A party is deemed to have cognizance of a fact if the party

1. has actual knowledge of it,
2. has received notice of it,
3. ought reasonably to know it,
4. knows about a related or associated fact, or
5. would have known by making reasonable enquiries about it.

1.3.4. Maps

Essentially, maps give area information and fill in as source material for such data. Its motivation is to demonstrate the patterns of the world's physical and human highlights, radically decreased in size for concentrate in one spot. As per Brown most significant sorts of data made accessible from guide is -

- Surface highlights, for example, waterways, fields, mountains and other land or water structures.
- Places and their area or good ways from one another.
- Scientific information, for example, development of air masses, ocean currents or geographical formations.
- Social or social information, for example, populace or language pattern.
- Political information, for example, limits between states or nations, sorts of government or election result.

- Economic information, for example, industrial production, farming products or exchange transactions among countries

Any of this data can be appeared on either maps or globes. Globes, nonetheless, more often than not contain just political data and surface highlights. Maps are altogether different from books and periodicals: the cutting edge type has no writer, and now and again they have no genuine title. Dates are all the time lacking, and on account of remote maps it isn't in every case simple to recognize the piece of the world delineated. The issue of orchestrating them and recording them in a manner which will abuse them completely are confused by the various structures which they take the size, yet in addition in introduction, some are divider maps, others are globes, some are roller maps, very separated from the minor issues of altogether different maps being imprinted on the two sides of a similar sheet or various significant inset maps being incorporated into a heedless style.

There are a few techniques through which maps can be put away. The flat strategy for documenting guide is anyway less satisfactory than the vertical technique. In any case, inferable from the shallow drawers, a bureau for flat recording - regardless of whether of wood or steel- has as much space dedicated to parcels as to real guide space. In the second, it is simpler to separate and supplant a guide from a vertical than from a level position and maps of various sizes can be documented together vertically with no risk of the littler maps is being ignored.

Collison recommends that smaller map books can be recorded on standard bookshelves, yet bigger map books of folio or more noteworthy size ought to ideally be documented on a level plane, and on profound racking of the roller type to encourage pull back and substitution. Bigger maps are frequently suspended from the roof or dividers, being unrolled by ropes at eye-level. A superior framework is to store them moved up in vertical compartments rather like huge umbrella stands, or to record them on a level plane in profound retires in cabinets. Edges of maps ought to be bound with fabric or tape by a unique edge-binding machine.

1.3.5. Audiovisual Material

The innovative advances, and specifically the new media and formats for recording data, has requested the improvisation of new procedures and strategies for taking care of data. Bookkeepers and chroniclers have not thought that it was anything but difficult to adapt to the changes. Broad media materials in libraries and archives have accordingly to a huge degree experienced both physical and scholarly disregard. It is just inside the most recent decade or so the acknowledgment has started to first light that various media materials are a significant part inside the general data arrange and that more consideration ought to be paid to these materials both to guarantee their preservation and to upgrade their abuse as wellspring of data.

Peter Mazikana saw that the approach and advance of new innovation and of the new data media have not been uniform all through the world. The preservation of broad media materials requires an organized and supported methodology at institutional, national and global levels. There are as of now in presence national, worldwide and non-administrative associations worried about varying media materials. The worldwide Federation of Television Archives (FIAT), the International Film and Television board (IFTC), the International alliance of Film Archives (FIAF), the International Association of sound Archives (lASA), the International Federation of Library Associations (IFLA), the International committee of Archives (ICA), and various others at national and local levels.

The preservation of varying media materials requires the proper gear for examination, rewinding, re-tensioning or move to new materials and new formats.

1.3.6. Gramophone Records

Robert Collison has taken a broad audit of storage types of gear and techniques for exceptional materials in libraries the most punctual mode for the account of sound was the chamber, developed by Thomas Edison in 1877, and by 1888 a few American firms were advertising chambers containing music or spoken introductions. Gramophone Records, inferable from their structure, arrangement and delicacy, should be secured against practically every one of the adversaries of libraries-fire, water, heat, rubbing, harsh taking care of, weight and inordinate development, are for the most part dangers which must be made preparations for. Records are best retired vertically in overwhelming manila envelopes on racks partitioned by dainty swaggers at interims of 7 inches or less. They ought to be documented near one another with the goal that they stand upstanding and yet are not very tight. It is common to have separate grouping for the different sizes - 10 inches, 12 inches and so forth. The appearance of long-playing records which need much more prominent security against mileage has been met in the United States by the arrangement of individual record holders comprising of intense pressboard covers with level spines and adjusted corners, to these solid art paper envelopes are connected by methods for gummed restricting strips. The envelope opens within to keep the record from sneaking out.

Gramophone records can't be documented like books, and they can't be listed with as much speed than or very as effectively as either books or music. Their treatment requires a totally new methodology with respect to the custodian. Their dealing with an ordering prompts new issues, which need cautious arrangement. In this manner a book or a volume of music can for the most part be viewed as a homogeneous entire, behind whose aggregation lays a positive arrangement or reason. That isn't the situation for gramophone records, where the music one side of the circle may have no association with that on the opposite side.

Gramophone records, inferable from their structure and the materials of which they are created, just as their delicacy, should be ensured against every one of the adversaries of the libraries. It very well may be by and large said that gramophone records are harmed by ecological components; for example dampness, intemperate warmth, contamination and somewhat development of parasites, harsh taking care of, weight and extreme development. They ought to be best retired vertically in overwhelming manila envelopes on racks controlled warmth and moistness is fundamental for long haul conservation of these materials.

1.3.7. Filmstrips

The Filmstrips has frequently been designated, "a heedful in a handful". This depiction is adept since what could be compared to a hundred charts, pictures, drawings, or content cards can be set on a length of film, twisted into a roll and set in a holder roughly 1 inch in measurement and 1½ inches high. This compilation of thoughts and sources into such little space results, frequently, in practically identical reserve funds in expenses of generation and publication.

Filmstrips are made out of a progression of still pictures and titles or descriptions put in consecutive request on 35mm film from 2 to 6 feet long, with sprocket openings on each side. They are usually somewhere in the range of twenty and fifty edges (singular pictures) long, despite the fact that they might be up to 100 casings. Filmstrips are delivered in high contrast or shading. James Brown referenced a portion of the usual purposes for utilizing filmstrips are: -

- To give a premise to observing signs.
- To help explaining abilities for example "flow to" filmstrips are normal.
- To give data.
- To invigorate artistic appreciation.
- To create enthusiasm for further quest for subject.

Filmstrips are normally all around secured by their individual metal covers, and need simply to be kept in a sheltered spot. The shape and size of the compartments producers their storage on racks inadmissible and uneconomical, and filmstrips are thusly best documented in shallow boxes or drawers fitted with allotments or formed bars to hold the canisters in position.

1.3.8. Films

The film empowers an instructor to re-make in the study hall occasions, activities, or procedures happening anyplace on the planet whenever. Through, the film, some "genuine" encounters might be shared by each understudy and watcher, and the impairments of time, size, and separation might be survived. Coordinated utilization of instructive films with other instructional materials offer a proficient methods for improved learning in a wide assortment of study hall circumstances. Attributes of films are as underneath:-

- Films consolidate "sight in movement" with different sounds to follow up on two faculties at any given moment.
- Films constrain consideration using movement and coordinated sight in a semi obscured room.
- Films can help get over significant scholarly obstructions to learning.
- Films help to re-make the past.
- Films give normal encounters.
- Films give a congruity of activity.

- The primary enthusiasm of a film in many kinds of libraries is in its subject. In most of libraries the possessions of films are exceptionally little. Their shapes and substance deny them of the full energy about their genuine worth. The strategy along these lines, ought to be to abuse their one of a kind characteristics to the most extreme, while simultaneously saving a daily practice, which secure them enough and adds as meager as conceivable to crafted by a bustling staff. Curators need to know much of the significant sorts of films.

The storage of films presents new issues; as a matter of first importance, their shape, size and substance make it basic that they ought to be put away on a level plane. Furthermore, there is the increased risk of fire accidents, which is best met by putting away films in metal containments, or in asbestos - lined drawers, which can be shut and bolted; it must be recalled too that films are once in a while appeared in the library itself, their presentation includes their being moved to different places in appropriate holders. The unsteady idea of films, and particularly the inflammability and intrinsic concoction unsteadiness of nitrate film base things, should be remembered. Usual check-up of the films ought to be made with the goal that any indications of decay might be recognized before the harm ends up broad.

1.3.9. Microfilm

Micrographic was designed from the beginning in 1839; in any case, it's utilization in libraries began in late 1930s when libraries started making microfilm duplicates of uncommon reports for open use and furthermore started changing over paper documents to microfilm as a methods for saving extra room and protecting newsprint, which for the most part has a fast decay rate in its unique structure by the 1950s, there was a boundless acknowledgment that microfilm could be utilized not just for the preservation of back records and curiously large reports, however an essential piece of dynamic data frameworks. As indicated by John Avedon micropublishing is a communications method, which uses photographic procedures to scale down printed or graphic material. It includes four stages.

(a) Photographing the material

(b) Copying or imitating the microcopies for conveyance.

(c) Recovering put away miniaturized scale pictures by methods for manual or programmed gadget, and

(d) Showing pictures on a reader screen for review and utilizing a reader printer for creating printed copies

Commission on Preservation and Access saw that contrasted and other present day data media, microfilm has the favourable position that the material experiences no major specialized change and is in this way "future-proofed". The simple put away data is legitimately available, with generally little exertion, to the human eye. Expanding national and global similarity of microfilming frameworks guarantees acknowledgment crosswise over national fringes. Microforms can be financially made, copied, and conveyed. Microfilm frameworks can be joined with electronic information preparing (edp) get to frameworks. Yet, microfilm can likewise be proficiently digitized with microfilm scanners. This will turn out to be progressively affordable as the generation quality and monetary feasibility of advanced access procedures improve.

Microforms are a truly feasible approach to save data. Recorded perpetual quality can be given when required; be that as it may, the lasting quality of the picture depends not only on utilizing the film, yet in addition on the way in which it is handled and put away. Microfilms can be influenced by the mugginess of the environment, yet the level of changelessness acetic acid derivation microfilm is equivalent to that of paper given reasonable storage, stickiness and temperature conditions. Perfect conditions for microfilm incorporate storage in metal-for the most part aluminum-holders, when not being used. The standard development of a reasonable compartment is portrayed in the British standard Institution's storage of microfilm.

REVIEW QUESTIONS

1. Define Conservation and preservation.
2. What are the methods in conservation and preservation?
3. Stages involved in evolutions of writing materials?
4. List out all inherent characteristics of the library materials.

2

Hazards to Library Materials

LEARNING OBJECTIVES

After reading this unit, you will be able to

- Explain the Environmental Factors.
- Explain the biological factors which are hazards to library materials.
- Explain the chemical factors used in production and preservation of documents.

2.1. ENVIRONMENTAL FACTORS - TEMPERATURE, HUMIDITY, LIGHT AND DUST

Introduction

Studies specify that cooler temperatures be located for library resources. According to Library of preservation references, a perfect atmosphere for books is 55^0 F storage capacities. Miscellaneous use storage abilities must be retained at 70^0 F. If library properties are retained distinctly from usage zones, the temperature can be carried down further to 65^0 F or less. Mechanical damage can cause uncontrolled moisture levels. If any chance that conditions is excessively humid, material will swell and twist, bringing about cockling and other physical contortions. These dimensional changes debilitate physical bonds and set up stresses that can abbreviate the life of generally materials. In the event that conditions are excessively dry, materials will end up weak and increasingly vulnerable to breaking, especially during handling. Light is crucial in the arrangement of library administrations since materials must be recognized and read. Then again, it is perhaps the greatest enemies of library materials, particularly paper. Evans (1995) clarified that non-print materials are especially delicate with the impacts of bright light, so tapes and microforms should never be retired close to a window.

The care and handling of library material for persons and organizations with little or no understanding of conservation does not provide a extensive list of detailed techniques and practices, but provides fundamental data to help libraries adopt a responsible position to take care of their collections. Collection threats are often recognized, although the implications of ignoring the hazards are often not sufficiently loudly declared by librarians.

Therefore,' IFLA Principles on the Care and Handling of Library Materials ' aims to encourage those accountable to face these implications and to formulate a favorable strategy for the future of content in their collections together with scientific and technical specialists.

Exposing the vulnerability of library materials will promote the accurate management and treatment of library materials. The following books include extensive bibliographies on subjects covered briefly in this publication. It is suggested that readers learn more about them.

Often the word ' preservation' contains everything necessary to protect the well-being of the library collection, whether managerial, administrative, financial or personal. In this document, however, the maintenance implies the provision of an adequate level of safety, environmental inspection, storage, care and handling, delaying further chemical deterioration and preventing physical harm to library material.

The' preservation' of library material was deliberately ruled out. Whereas many preservation options can be implemented by non-specialists, only trained experts who have access to suitable equipment and materials are able to perform conservation. Conservation is also a work-intensive and expensive practice that few organizations can afford worldwide. This document therefore concentrates exclusively on actions that can be taken by the majority of libraries to avoid and slow the degradation of their collections.

A broad variety of organic products including paper, cloth, animal skin, and adhesives can be found in traditional library collection. The natural ageing process of such organic substances is continuous and unavoidable. It is difficult to stop this damage completely, although steps can be taken to slow this deterioration by managing it carefully and offering a friendly atmosphere. The chemical and physical stability of the library materials also relies on the quality and handling, in combination with the design and construction of the final device, of the raw products used in its production.

Over the decades, mass manufacturing pressures have decreased material quality in libraries. Many of the paper stock produced after 1850 is extremely acidic, breaks and destroys itself on time. For the sake of automation, binding methods have been abbreviated and many text blocks are now only kept by adhesive together. Indeed, all books, especially leather bindings, are significantly more likely to be harmful than most. Modern media such as microforms, optical and magnetic disks, digital formats, pictures, audio and visual media all suffer from inherent conservation issues and must be properly stored and used when not prematurely destroying them. It is frequently hard to recognize that many library materials reach the end of their natural lives and can only be extended by careful storage and processing in the few years that they have left.

Why keep? Why maintain it?

The sort and use of the library represent its collection's conservation requirements.

Obviously, the conditions of conservation of the local government credit library differ from that of a national library. However, for a few years or indefinitely, both are required to keep and keep their collections accessible.

Libraries cannot economically allow themselves to wear their holdings early. Even if possible, substitute library material is costly. Conservation is economically meaningful.

- What will be of interest for researchers in the future cannot be readily anticipated.
- The best way to serve potential customers is to preserve present collections.
- The competent and professional library personnel should commit themselves to the care and preservation of the material they operate with.

Bibliography materials deterioration is a consequence of the intervention of library officials. In the majority of instances, the substance that contains library materials promotes degradation. Which potential agents are present to shorten the helpful life of products determines the particular place and climate in the library. Marrow defined the few library material deteriorating agents that are light, heat, moisture. Gas Air Pollution, fungi, insects, human beings and disasters in specific.

On the other side, Alegbeleye (2002) obviously says that the use of preservation and conservation is rarely misconceived. He describes the interchangeable terms conservation and conservation. However, specialists in the field draw a difference between the two phrases in a strict way. The conservation of library materials and the archival information involves all management and financial considerations including arrangements for storage and housing, staff, policy, technology and techniques engaged in preservation. Conservation, on the contrary, relates to particular methods used to slow deterioration by directly interfering in physical or chemical make-up and prolong the life of an item. The latter include the repair, binding or de-acidification of damaged books. From the above explanation, we would deduce that the conservation of library material relates either in their initial physical format or in any other format to operations relating to the conservation of library material. This involves a number of procedures from environmental control to therapy for preservation.

The therapy of library products is therefore necessary to stabilize their physical composition in order to sustain their survival in their initial format as long as possible.

Preservation at a greater level means far more than maintaining the material in its initial form or familiarizing itself with every formatting technology. It implies accessibility, too. If you need it, you get it. It does. The entire safety, shelving, shelf reading and distribution method are therefore methods of conservation.

The core of libraries is materials. They are essential access to teaching and data, and they maintain understanding in the future and enable previous interpretation. Every library, big or small, should have a well-defined conservation programme. Users and employees should be conscious of their role in the conservation program in planning for preventive conservation. S.R. S.R. Ranganathan claims that "books are to be used" in one of his five library laws. If the materials are not well maintained, they cannot perform this task, for preventing or delaying decay is the most efficient way of establishing longevity of books / materials. There is no contradiction in the fact that data is as old as the age of humanity, so it is extremely important that information sources be adequately preserved and conserved for the intellectual, political, social, cultural and posterity spheres of human development.

Having seen preservation and conservation in an overall sense, and have seen the need for measures to be intended in order to preserve a reasonable standardization compared to that which is generally obtainable, it is imperative that they are kept free of dust in maintaining media materials / documents. They should be cleaned and taken care of properly. Massive damage to any media can be caused by dust.

Elaturoti (1982) said that media materials that can soak books and other printed materials must be prevented from using water. It can also lead to corroding audio-visual devices. Insecticides should be used cautiously because they can cause non-book material harm.

Due to limited resources and the state of preservation in most libraries, all documents or recorded materials cannot be kept in their initial format or transferred to other media for conservation even intellectual content. It is essential to select and prioritize.

Cooperation is essential to effective projects for conservation. No library is able to preserve all. Mass therapy methods such as book and paper DE acidification are created through collaboration. In North America and Europe co-operative programs for the preservation of valid microfilm collection were effective. The European Registry of Microfile Masters (EROMM) and the enhanced bibliography control supported by the Internet are today working together to protect the documentary patrimony. In fact, the conservation and transfer of electronically productive optical digital techniques offers a solution as well as actual obstacles to maintaining documentary heritage (Feather and Sturges, 1997). In addition, libraries should not only obtain the materials but should also guarantee the conservation and conservation of the purchased materials in usability for generations of customers.

Libraries should be air-conditioned because they cannot overemphasize their significance to library products. While there are sometimes no possible damages to library equipment, but careful preventive measures may reduce or prevent material deterioration, as the old adage says: "prevention is better than treatment."

2.1.1. Light

Light is the type of emission that any individual can grasp; emission is estimated in wavelength. Wavelengths of infrared radiation, visible and ultraviolet are possible deteriorative specialists inside a library atmosphere. The wavelength is shorter, the extra powerful effect of the radiation. Radiation is a type of energy that advances weakening by enacting chemical responses. The base energy a sub-atomic must get so as to peruse is 'activation energy'. Activation energy is distinctive to explicit materials, and response won't happen if the activation energy for a material is not come to. Light is extremely compelling wellspring of activation energy.

Since it is visibly hard to repel light from library materials, some weakening is unavoidable. The standard of correspondence expresses that by controlling contact to light one can control the amount of weakening. This should be possible either by controlling the sort and measure of light (the intensity) or by controlling to what extent an article is presented to light. This rule is especially significant in the presentation of uncommon and one of a kind material. It very well may be outlined by the formula:

Total exposure = Time × Intensity.

There are three causes of enlightenment regular to libraries-normal light coming in through skylights and windows, forbidden fluorescent lights and radiant bulbs. The quality and consistency of the light are likewise significant contemplations. It is commonly comprehended that more prominent forces of light (in excess of 35 foot-candles) are a bit much or attractive in libraries and add to eye fatigue.

2.1.2. Heat

Like light, heat is a type of energy that endorses weakening. Temperature is a proportion of the force of heat energy. The higher the temperature, the quicker the library materials will fall apart. The typical standard guideline is that for each 10°C (18°F) ascent in temperature, the pace of chemical reaction doubles. In any case, the pace of chemical responses in cellulose (paper and cloth duplicates for each 5°C (9°F) increase in temperature.

Libraries cannot keep materials in consistent, all out obscurity; they cannot store materials forever at very low temperatures. In this way weakening from the impact of warmth is inescapable. Libraries be that as it may, can fundamentally lessen the pace of crumbling by bringing down temperature. Library materials put away at 70°F will decay around half as quick as library materials put away at 79°F. Any material made out of natural materials that are effectively oxidized ought to be put away at as low a temperature as is pragmatic. This will lessen the warmth prompted energy of the particles and hinder the degradation procedure.

Variances in temperature are unfortunate in light of the fact that numerous library materials are comprised of a few segment materials that assimilate heat. Fast and successive changes in temperature will cause pressure that prompts auxiliary breakdown.

2.1.3. Humidity

The capacity of air to hold dampness is subject to temperature since hotter air can bolster more dampness. In view of this reliance, humidity is normally stated as a level of the most extreme measure of water the air could hold at a specific. Marrow [24] has given the underneath referenced equation measure remedy the relative moistness (RH)

RH = Amount of water in a given nature of air/ Maximum measure of water that the air can hold at that temperature * 100%

In a fixed compartment, for example, a show case or dispatching holder, the measure of water vapour noticeable all around stays steady with the goal that build-up can without much of a stretch structure if the temperature is raised or then again brought down and raised.

Water goes about as a physical specialist of disintegration by making hygroscopic materials experience dimensional changes. At the point when RH rises, moisture is reabsorbed. This procedure of development and compression can make library materials break separated physically. This sort of physical pressure is exacerbated by the way that diverse segment materials ingest moisture at various rates and in various sums.

2.1.4. Gaseous Air Pollution

The fossil fuel are burned (petroleum, Oil, coal , and natural gas) which causes gaseous air pollutions in industrial area and cities. It is these centralizations of man-made poisons that advance the decay of social property in libraries and historical centres of their contaminations; sulphur dioxide is a main deteriorative cause.

At the point when petroleum derivatives are singed, sulphur polluting influences join with oxygen to frame sulphur dioxide (SO2). Since S02 is promptly assimilated on surfaces, luckily, the fixation inside is only one-portion of what it is outside. Yet, in industrial and urban regions, that one-half is a major focus.

2.1.5. Particulate matter

Dust, dirt, sand and smoke are significant hazards for soiling and abrading of the library materials, facilitating the action of water and organic agents, as well as transporting and combining them with gaseous pollutants.

Mechanical action–dust created by a melting method or by fine sand odder dirt straight into the air–constitutes the biggest particulate matter. The lowest information consists of chemical processes or incomplete combustion of fuels. Those tiny particles stay suspended in the air until such time as a dust film can be accessed and used, for instance, on a surface.

2.2. BIOLOGICAL FACTORS–FUNGI, INSECT AND OTHER PARASITES

Mold, mildew can cause severe harm to paper products, which are often irreparable. Silver fish, bookworms, booklices, and cockroaches are the most prevalent species influencing library and archival material. Most insects are not appealed to the paper but rather to dark, humid, dirty, clustered, uninterrupted sizing, adhesive and starch sizings. Mold and mould are fungal kinds, micro-organisms which are sustenance dependent on other organisms. Molds excrete enzymes that enable them to digest, alter and weaken organic materials, such as paper and book bindings. Harvey (1993) proposed a clean, well-ventilated and climate-controlled atmosphere to prevent any of these pests.

2.2.1. Fungi

Fungi are a big and varied group; "mold" and "mildew" are referred to as non-parasitary tiny fungi.

Coloured patterns and blotches generally seem as a fluid gray layer in libraries. Fungi function as biological agents of decay and cause weakening and decomposition to ingest organic materials. The mushrooms are very patient. They are very resistant to adverse circumstances and will just wait for circumstances to resume development. Specimens of herbariums are known to stay feasible for 26 years. Fungi are a risk to library equipment at all times.

2.2.2. Insects

Library material is highly hazardous to insects. They quickly ingest paper, cloth, leather, vellum and parchment, and paste and glue. Detections are hard because they depend on the harm being identified and many insects operate in rarely visited places or at nocturnal times. Some insects only feed on the ground, soften and weaken, while others create sophisticated tunnels. Others just eat paste and glue.

2.2.3. People

Human humans are degrading agents and librarians and bookbinders are at the top of the list. As policymakers, librarians are directly accountable for their collections as a whole. In addition, library users, by their instance, learn how library materials are treated. Librarians establish environmental management norms; select services such as binding and reprography; and define shelving and circulation strategies. They can behave inadvertently as agents for deterioration through failure to address conservation and conservation issues.

Based on inappropriate use, library materials are also deteriorating. Library personnel and employers may, by misuse of library materials, inadvertently cause harm. Declining intentional abuse is also occurring. Despite the priority of employers ' service, careless and selfish conduct will happen in the library. The materials of the library should be used. Simple wear and tear is essentially inevitable. Well-meaning but inadequate therapy could lead to structural deterioration and breakdown. Inadequate measures are not only a nuisance; data can be obscured and destructed and money can definitely be wasted.

2.2.4. Disasters

Disasters are a constant danger to the products of libraries. No library is immune to natural or man-made disasters that might happen.

A collection may be completely destroyed by fire. Nearby items that are not straight flamed can be irreparably soot and smoke charred or demolished. Fire heat creates shrinking and warp bindings and the melting of plastic foundation materials. Water used to fight a fire can generally harm both the water itself and the strength of high-pressure hoses. Fire and heat are also the major agents of deterioration in the water, as well as fire and heat, floods, tornadoes and heavy rain storms, snow flows and roof leaks. Flood-borne dirt and debris can be embedded in equipment and can make rescue and recovery extremely complicated. Wet book absorbs water and swells and jams in racks.

2.3. CHEMICAL FACTORS–CHEMICAL SUBSTANCES USED IN THE PRODUCTION AND CONSERVATION OF DOCUMENTS

The conservation of library products may be jeopardized by airborne contaminants in the form of gasses and particulates. Photocopiers, paintings, cleaning equipment, untreated wood and certain adhesives and plastics can produce gaseous pollutants on the indoor environment. Pollution in particular is also a major problem. Particles are made from smoke, dust, and car motors in the form of small, strong substances. The library should be completely air-conditioned and extremely recommended for books with air conditioners. Climate systems assist to stabilize libraries ' temperature and moisture. They also contribute towards filtering out particles and chemicals.

Emergency Procedures During Fire Accidents

Immediately evacuate the building when there is a fire or when there are fire alarms. It is up to each employee to be acquainted with the evacuation procedure in their library.

Procedure

1. Remain calm.
2. Upon a fire or a fire alarm sound, evacuate the building immediately. Leave the light on. Leave the light on.
3. In all libraries there are fire alarms. This is turned on if smoke is detected in a library building via a smoke detector or by a beam detector. Alarms are tracked every 24 hours and when the alarm is sounding fire trucks are dispatched automatically. There are fire alarms all over the construction (as opposed to elevator alarms, boiler alarms, etc. located). When needed and secure, personnel can confirm that an alarm is a fire alarm by inspecting the noise from a fire alarm device.
4. *Fire extinguishers* : Only use extinguishers when fire is tiny and fast (such as fire in a trash bottle).
5. *Fire extinguisher instructions* : Taken pin, aim at the flaming base, squeeze handles together, and sweep with side to side movements (PASS). Sweep with the fire extinguisher.

   Make sure the fire is extinguished entirely.

   If your ability to extinguish the fire remains uncertain, do not try.

   Immediately escape the construction.
6. *Do Not Take Elevators* : Two personnel members, if

possible, should bring someone on crutches, in wheelchairs or for any other reason not in a position to bring the stairs to the stairway exit. If you don't have smoke in the stairwell, enter the stairwell. Ensure a secure closing of the door. Staff must leave the staircase individual to secure assistance.

Trust that the fire department will send fire fighting personnel to help the individual in the wheelchair (or on crutches) if evacuation is essential. An employee shall inform the fire department of where the individuals are waiting immediately. An employee should never jeopardize himself.

7. If there are too many people to wait in the exit hallway at the landing stage, look for another shelter area on the ground, such as the door room, window and telephone.
8. Use the following fire survival skills to protect yourselves:
   (a) Block door or winding openings where smoke could enter with towels or clothes. Put on your mouth and nose a moist cloth if necessary.
   (b) Put a signal in the window-something you'll notice (e.g. a large signal, or knot tied curtains).
   (c) Called emergency to report your place when smoke or fire enters the region. Keep to the ground to breathe the best air.
   (d) Don't open the windows or crack them. Smoke often enters through open windows from the outside of the building. Breaking window threatens you from the outside to get smoke and undermines the rescue attempts.
   (e) Library personnel should NOT try to transport persons who are unable to walk through stairs without endangering stairwell circumstances.
9. Report to the meeting location established. The

evacuation procedures for the library are required.

10. Do not return to the building until the suitable employees has instructed (normally Fire Department employees; building safety personnel or managers at certain places).
11. Without immediate danger, a double employee remainders close to the front door to prevent the arrival of people in the building.
12. Notify the Fire Department, the Library Manager, and the Library Director, the Assistant Director, or the Community Relations Manager about all incendiary or incidents, even if the fire is small and has extinguished. If you suspect that a fire might be incendiary (e.g., book drop burning materials, etc.), do not disturb the region unless staff from the Fire Department investigate.

Winter Storms

If the impending winter weather presents a risk to employees, employers, or library assets, the Library Manager may change working hours for a location. For general instructions, see the Regulations Manual.

Winter weather in the library district can cause travel to be dangerous or may influence working circumstances.

Procedures

1. *Potential hazards* : Be alert to potential hazards when high winds, snow or icy conditions are expected, such as:
   - (a) snow or ice covered parking lot or sidewalks
   - (b) broken window or door glass
   - (c) downed power lines
   - (d) downed or dangling tree limbs
   - (e) frozen pipes
   - (f) flying debris

2. To monitor the scenario, use common sense and rational judgment.
3. If the building has been harmed or if the property is in danger, call the Library Manager / Supervisor and Assistant Director.

?????? Something Missing Here

Procedures

1. Earthquakes, volcanoes, floods, etc. require attention from the natural emergencies. We will follow community emergency plans instead of comprehensive guidelines.
2. Earthquakes, flash floods, landslides and mudflows, thunderstorms, tsunamis, ash drop and acid rain are all disaster-related causes of volcanoes. Since volcanic eruptions can cause many miles of damage, our communities are likely to be evacuated.
3. In the unlikely case of such events, Community emergency plans will be pursued.

Moving the Materials

For the height and angle of view the document holder should be stable and adjustable.

The document holder should be positioned near to the screen at the same height and distance to decrease the tension of the head, neck and back of the screen. If the document is too high or does not fit a document holder, if space is accessible, it can be supported at an angle from the keyboard to the screen.

When you lift, bend or push, use adequate body mechanics. Train to think before lifting and stretching before working. If you need to raise your stance, follow the instructions below:

Procedures

1. Planning and testing your lift. Think of the product, before you lift, and ask, "Can I lift it alone? You know?"Is one person too awkward?"Is the way obvious?"You must also check the load to see how heavy it is before you lift.
2. Ask for assistance. For help, if the charge is too heavy or too unwilling to lift.
3. Get a solid base. Keep your feet apart, build a stable foundation and show your toes.
4. Bend your ankles.-Bend your knees. Don't bend at the waist. Don't bend at waist. Maintain the principles of leverage always in mind.
5. Strengthen the muscles of your stomach. When lifting offsetting the strength of the load, use intra-abdominal stress to help the spine. Exercise your muscles to cooperate.
6. Lift with your legs. After you have secured a good grip with your hands, let your leg muscles do the work of lifting. Do not depend on muscles in the weaker back.
7. Maintain closing the load. Bring the load to your body as close as possible. The nearer the spine is, the less the strength the back strength it exerts. Stay focused on your feet for your weight. Tuck your arms and elbows into your side.
8. Stay straight with your back. Do not add the weight of your body to the load resulting from bending over, either by lifting or loading. Do not twist.

2.3.1. The Need to Preserve and Conserve

Library materials are the fundamental issue of libraries, and the conservation demands arise. The value of documents in the form of their educational, socio-political and economic impact on society needs to be adequately taken into account when preserving the materials and how long each class of documents may have been kept for use and subsequently destroyed or preserved permanently for future use. But there is no infinite library material. They themselves are prone to decay and are therefore very important to preserve and preserve them. The preservation, preservation or impacts of both operations are needed to maintain the data contained in all communication media for the efficient use by future generations. Titles with contemporary, biographical or intellectual values need to be preserved. It is useful to note, for example, that paper is rapidly deteriorating due to its ephemeral nature. Machine-built paper is produced out of wood and contains pulp with damaging acids, which quickly worsen it. Binding materials also contain deteriorating damaging components. Increasing numbers of customers in open-accès repositorys cause deterioration and objects harm to highly precious products by environmental considerations such as elevated temperature and relative humidity, light exposure, air pollution and careless handling.

In the process of choices on preservation and conservation, three primary variables are crucial. It is:

(i) The building : define possible safety, fire, flood and other natural disasters hazards. The building:

(ii) Inside construction : read and watch regions, environmental and physical conditions of the shelving units, light levels, temperature and moisture measurements and air pollution assessments and iii. The collection: to identify the extent of paper damages, including paper bits, insect or mould harm and binding harm, etc.

REVIEW QUESTIONS

1. Define an Environmental, Biological and Chemical factor that is hazards to library materials.
2. Steps involved in environmental factors?
3. Steps involved in biological factors?
4. Steps involved in chemical factors?

3

Preventive Methods of Preservation of Library Resources

LEARNING OBJECTIVES

After reading this unit, you will be able to

- Explain the preventive measures for environmental, biological and chemical factors.
- State the disaster preparedness/response in preventive methods
- Explain care & handling, and methods involved in care & Handling of library resources.

INTRODUCTION

The goals and aims of every library are its own. But the library's fundamental function is to serve society as a communication medium. Library is a social organization which acquires and organizes and preserves data systematically in such a way that it is easy for users to use. The preservation of the documentary heritage that the library offers is part of every librarian's duty to guarantee access to the current and future generations. Bibliographic conservation is as ancient as a human civilization. Knowledge is documented, maintained and made accessible before the invention of paper in different formats and in different shapes.

A library is a repository of the knowledge of excellent past and current thinkers. It is a social institution responsible for the dissemination without discrimination of information to the individuals. The libraries have an invaluable legacy, preserving in numerous fields, ages and directions facts, ideas, achievements and evidence of human growth. Past documents are a natural resource and are essential for both the current and future generations. Any losses in this type of materials cannot be replaced. Consequently, not only scholarly dedication b is to preserves this intellectual cultural heritage.

Preservation is the method by which all library resources are taken care to maintain in a fairly healthy state so that our posterity can use them. There are two conservation elements –

(i) Preventive preservation and

(ii) Curative preservation

1. Preventive preservation : These are indirect actions designed to raise the life expectancy of the library's assets undamaged or yet damaged. It includes all excellent housekeeping, cleaning and dusting techniques, regular surveillance and avoidance of physical, chemical, biological and other damages possible.

2. Curative Preservation : Curative conservation comprises of all types of direct activities to increase the life expectancy of the library records without damages or damages.

Causes of deterioration of library documents

We understand that most of the library materials are in paper. Deterioration changes the originality of the library papers, the paper has a powerful cellulose bond at the beginning and this bond is loosened and the paper turns yellow. There are three categories for causes of deterioration - Natural Ageing, Intrinsic or inherent factors, External conditions.

Natural Ageing

The durability of the materials is affected by the natural aging through gradual decay or degradation.

Intrinsic or inherent factors : Inherent factor means the fundamental constituents used in the making of physical objects of library materials as well as development processes.

External Conditions : External conditions include various environmental, chemical, biological, human and library documents that damage them.

This study focuses only on environmental variables together with the manner they are conserved.

3.1. PREVENTIVE MEASURES FOR ENVIRONMENTAL FACTORS

The environment consists of living organisms (such as crops, livestock and human beings), physical environments (for air, water and soil) and meteorological elements (for example, temperature, sunshine, moisture, wind velocity and average precipitation) are the third elements. The physical environment components are mainly accountable for determining a region's climate factor. Light, heat, humidity and water and pollutants such as dust, dirt, fumes etc.. The major environmental variables influence the physical deterioration of paper-based library products.

Light : Light is a damaging factor for paper and associated lighting materials. The deterioration of paper is caused by natural and artificial light. The strength of the organic material of information resources may be destroyed by light, and the ink and colors decay. Every illuminating source that proliferates as a wave is a type of energy, radiated by light.

The ultra-violet Region : This region is split between the wavelengths 136A0 to 4000A0. This region lies in two areas called close and far ad whole.

Visible region : Range 4000 A0 to 8000 A0, also known as the region of white light. This area has seven colours: purple, indigo, blue, green, yellow, orange and red.

The Infra-Red Region : This area is also called Heat-Ray. This area is between 8000A0 to 4x106A0 wave lengths. Ultra-violet rays are typically considered destructive sources for library equipment. Writing may vanish entirely when exposed to light for a long time.

Heat : Heat impacts cloth, paper and other associated organic materials adversely. High atmospheric temperatures are usually the heat source. In the scale of Centigrade or Fahrenheit, heat is evaluated according to the temperature. High heat with low moisture leads cellulose fibers to dehydrate and the paper breaks down. Hot weather plays a hazardous part when the life of paper, books and associated products is weakened. The appropriate temperature should be provided to protect library material against decay.

Humidity & moisture : Humidity is the atmospheric air's moisture. The humidity is evaluated by relative moisture. Due to the organic object's absorption property, the moisture is absorbed at a elevated moisture level. High moisture leads insects to grow, while low moisture losses the flexibility of fabrics. For conservation of paper documents, a temperature of 200c–240c and a RH of 55% are most efficient.

A certain quantity of moisture is essential, but paper becomes soggy and the moisture weakens the fibers of paper in long-term, elevated humidity conditions. The root cause of multiple kinds of deterioration of physical, chemical or biological library products is moisture. It weakens the adhesive and loosens the book. The size of paper components is also weaker and the ink is spread. Moist book pages are often stuck together. The effect of paper is yellow and spots-faced also speeds up different kinds of chemical deterioration. Moisture also encourages fungal growth, which damages paper and books.

Pollutants : Man-made chemicals that release into the air, such as sulfur di-oxide, dust, dirt and smoke, are dangerous to cellulose. Dust is known as thin, dry particles of any matter in the air. Dust comprised, among other things, soil, tar, metallic materials, fungal spores and moisture. The stain and the dirt cause the library's collection to degrade both physically and chemically. As the dust is airborne, it sits on any object's surface. Dust is hygroscopic in nature, and it is converted into dirt when it is intermingled with elevated humidity and it becomes hard to remove if the dirt clinges to the books surface. Staub and dust are sources to degrade the library collection physically and physically. The dust functions as a moisture-collecting core and this humidity gives the needed moisture to increase the fungus and to produce chemical acid reactions. Due to the fact that dust and dirt are strong particles of different sizes and durability, they abrasion on the book surface.

Water : As physical agents of worsening, water undergoes dimensional changes causing hygroscopic materials. Water can come from sources such as natural disasters, neglect of human beings etc. Excess water generally appears as biological agent development. Like mushrooms or mushrooms etc. Water impacts include stained paper, red leather, battered ink, weakened adhesive, and durable fungi. Water also damages the roasting of steel furnishings.

Water damaging for the library collection may come from sources such as natural calamities, negligence on the part of humans, leak roofs, faulty plumbing and open doors during the rainy season. Excessive water causes biological attacks on paper, often expressed as fungal or mildew development.

Natural disaster

Environmental variables may include natural disasters. Natural disaster is an unexpected occurrence that jeopardizes library collections or archives. Object harm to library material is caused by natural calamities such as floods, fire, earth quakes and a building collapse. Desaster planning for libraries and archives, their employees and collections is a matter of fundamental safety. Natural catastrophes are rain and wind, flooding, earthquakes, fires, water, and chemical spills. In humid circumstances, mold starts to form quickly following floods. Audio-visual materials are vulnerable to water, such as photographs, microforms, magnetic media and other disks; damage depends on the material type, the exposure time of the material, the temperature, etc. Due to the effect of disasters on library collections, suitable preventive steps can be taken when the library building is built.

No library is exempt from the damage caused by natural or man-made disasters. There is a probability that the collections are organically produced in libraries, archives and Museums. When a fire begins, the materials that get fire are hard to save. Things not straight flamed, soot and smoke may be charred. Heat from the flames leads to shrink bindings, warp and the melting of plastic products.

3.1.1. Methods of Preservation for environmental factors

The process of keeping an object safe from harm or loss, damage, destruction or decay, and maintaining it in a reasonably sound condition for present and future use is called preservation. Preservation includes stabilizing, maintaining and monitoring temperature, humidity, light exposure, air pollution, dirt, dust and mold etc. Methods of preservation can be studied by two ways: Preventive Preservation, Curative preservation.

Preventive Preservation : Preventive conservation refers to those particular policies and procedures that protect library and archival materials against harm, decline and deterioration. It reduces the deterioration by taking preventive steps. Preventive conservation involves the use of paper and ink of excellent quality, excellent handling, storage and service, safeguarding the right environment and neutralizing acidity.

Traditional manuscripts are hand-written scripts from the early 4th to the 19th centuries. These handwritten records represent Myanmar's wealthy cultural heritage and elevated academic achievements. These cover a variety of literature, history, Buddhist religious doctrines, medicine and customs.

Our invaluable documentary patrimony, which must be maintained due to its irreplaceable nature, is traditional manuscripts. It is therefore essential that these intellectual legacies are maintained and developed due to their contents that give an abundance of information for an interpretation of the cultural history of Myanmar and its culture.

Preventive Measure for Environmental Condition : In order to maintain the library material correctly, the environmental condition or the storage condition should be scientifically monitored. Some considerations for environmental control are scientific construction with enough light, appropriate temperature ranges, humidity and the right use of furniture. In order to promote the conservation of organic library materials, environmental inspections are required. The humidity speeds down organic matter and spreads mildew and pests such as silverfish, termites, white ants etc. The most important environmental variables are relative moisture, pests, pollutants and light temperatures. Books and other materials are collected and then left sensitive to relative moisture. High moisture promotes mold development and infestations indoors. Low moisture causes loss of flexibility of materials. Relative moisture relates in particular to the quantity of water vapor in the atmosphere at certain temperatures.

Temperature can be described to evaluate the speed with which molecules move within materials. The faster molecules move at greater speed, so that heat accelerates deteriorating chemical reactions. A slower rate of deterioration could be at a reduced temperature.

The cleaning of library equipment and structures and furnishings is very important in order to preserve library records from deterioration. Ambient pollutants such as dust and acid gasses produce unhygienic conditions in recorded products and promote mildew development. Cleaning avoids chemical reactions on cellulosic materials and other materials used as binding by accumulation of dirt, dust, shoots, stains etc.

Deterioration : Deterioration is a change of original state of any material by interaction between the object and factors of destruction.

3.2. PREVENTIVE MEASURES FOR BIOLOGICAL AND CHEMICAL FACTORS

Bio-deterioration is commonly called the deterioration induced by biological agents such as micro-organisms, insects and rodents. Nearly all book parts used to bind are susceptible to attack by these bio-agents be it paper, leather, fabrics or straw boards. The problem of biodegradation is an important issue for the tropical warm and humid climate such as India. The climatic state accelerates living organisms' development and development. There is no library, perhaps, that has not endured the devastation of these biodegrading agents. These organic agents can be divided into

(i) Micro-organisms- Fungus or moulds, bacteria etc.

(ii) Insects

(iii) Rodents

(i) Micro-organisms

A. Fungus : Fungus is a large group of plant organisms that are heterogeneous. There are fungal spores in the earth, water and air and they stay in sleeping condition for many years. These spores are sprouting and growing when moisture and heat are needed. Fungi usually grow within 63-100 percent of relative humidity and 15-350c of temperature. Fungal growth in libraries is known as a mold or mildew and is found in paper, leather and fabrics as brown / black vegetative development. Cellulosis is consumed and nutrients in leather, sticks, binding threads, etc. also thrive in the funguses; they weaken and stain the paper and can cause discolouration.

B. Bacteria : Apart from the fungus, cellulose in paper and binding textiles are also decomposed in bacteria.

(ii) Insects

Although thousands of insects exist, the archive library materials only suffer serious harm to certain insects. Silvers, cockroaches, libraries, bookworms and termites.

A. Silverfish : These insects are principally supplied with foodstuffs such as starch, glue and gelatin used in papers as materials of sizing. The insects attract dust and dirt as well. They love the dark and only work at night. There are no leaves of silverfish, silver or pearl gray and 8 to 10 mm long. They eat the bottom of the paper and also eat billboards, envelopes and so on. They are growing in paper, prints, pictures, catalog cards and boxes of carton. The space for the egg laying in the dark on library shelves, in the Catalog cabinets and drawers.

B. Cockroaches : Brown or blackish brown colored cockroaches are frequent throughout the globe. They consume leaves of paper, bookbinding, textiles, etc. They are often discovered and are extremely active during the night in libraries, archives and museums. They live in wet corners, walls and floors, almonds, racks and wooden closets under and behind them. You excrete a dark brown fluid that leaves the paper stains and is hard to remove.

C. Book worms or Book beetles : Bookworms influence books and manuscripts very extensively. They feed on paper and cause extensive harm, as the name itself indicates. Bookworms in libraries lay their eggs at the book corners and on the bookbinding surface. In the pages and panels of the books they create tunnels.

D. Book lice : Dark dusty places filled with unused books, humidity and warmth are crucial for book like development. The color is gray or white. They injure book bindings by eating paste and glue and also eat the fungus that is created between the book's internal corners.

E. Termites or White Ants : In the tropical climate, the damage caused by termites to the library materials is considerable. The most appropriate place for termites is the wet or humid environment. They consume wood and paper and can attack any cellulose material. They can make irreparable harm in no moment when they begin to destroy the books. The attacked materials leave mud imprisonment.

They come from two classifications such as termites and termites. The termites live on the ground, and their mud tunnels on the walls, the bookcases, the furniture can be visited in the libraries. Wood termites live above the floor and enter the construction through cracks and openings.

(iii) Rodents

Mice, rats, squirrels, and many other species are included in rodents. Mice and rats are primarily discovered in bookstores and are entered through dry drains and door and window openings into houses. In libraries, materials made of paper, cloth, leather, glue, etc. are eaten and destroyed. These animals move and hide in dark corners very quickly.

3.2.1. Preventive Measures for Biological Factors

Because the stormy air, humidity, darkness and dingy locations in a library promote the development of biological pests, excellent home care is required to manage the propagation of the insects and maintain optimal storage conditions. Cross-windows, fans and exhaust fans ensure excellent air circulation, but at times air circulation is essential in the space with electric fans. In order to eliminate humidity, it is best to prevent contact between book shelves and walls (at least 15 cm from the walls). In order to avoid the likelihood of insect hiding in the park, crack and loose joints in the floor or wall. It should not be permitted to have food inside the library. Periodic insecticidal powder use in solution such as lindane under shelves and admirals on dark corner walls is a useful precautionary measure for insect avoidance. Para-dichlorobenzene is safe to use because it serves both as a repellent for insects and as an insecticide.

One easy exercise is to maintain naphthalene bricks on the shelves as the insects are prevented from reaching the book racks. Dry neem leaves, neem seed powder and camphor tablets attached to bags of the muslim should be placed inside the shelves for pest control. Anti-insect therapy should be applied to the foundations of all new library structures.

3.2.2. Chemical Factors

In the production of paper sometimes low-cellulose fibers are used and certain chemical compounds such as alum, rosin etc. are used to size paper that cause acidity and make it easier to deteriorate the paper over time.

Unwanted materials like carbon oxides, sulphide, nitrogen and hydrogen sulphides are also present in the atmosphere among different constituents. The library products are impacted because the chemicals are carried in by the moisture absorbed into the paper. Sulfur dioxides, oxides of nitrogen and ozone are the significant deleterious substances in the library products. The risk to cellulose products, such as paper and cloth, is sulfur dioxide. The brown and fragrant edges of the books induced by sulphur dioxide are the most common impact in libraries. Most nitrogen dioxide originates from car exhaust and becomes nitric acid when combined with oxygen and water. This nitric acid is very acidic and assaults the teeth in tin, cloth, paper and leather. Ozone serves as a strong organic destroyer. It fades the colors of the textile book and also the book binding materials such as leather, gelatin, glue and paste can damage the ozone in humid environments.

3.2.2.1. Preventive Measures for Chemical Factors

There is no external acidity in the paper material if air pollution is controlled. The air intake is filtered into the storage areas, which can be reached through a 24-hour air conditioning system, as one of the best ways to control air pollutants. Simple measures such as wrapping books and manuscripts in cloth or putting them in book containers without this facility will significantly reduce the pollution consequences. Books kept indoors are better protected than books kept outdoors. Documents stored in folders are safer than those kept in the open folder. Save books and records from dust with proper care. For dusting racks and books, it is better to use vacuum cleaners and good brushes. There should be no direct use of chemical formulations for the book covers because they can have an negative impact on books, book users and library employees. Wood storage, which produces volatile acidic vapours, should be prevented. To be used, coats of acrylic emulsion paint must be applied. In order to re-pair and restore the records, acid free paper, board and excellent quality equipment should also be used.

3.3. DISASTER PREPAREDNESS/RESPONSE

Disaster leads to disastrous death and property loss in a community triggered by nature or by human events. This is a disastrous event that comes from either the wrath of the nature or human folly that leads to extensive harm, destruction, ecological disturbance, the loss of human lives, human pain, degraded health facilities and a large-scale reaction to mitigate and mitigate the extent of the suffering caused by extraordinary outside the impacted communities or areas Disasters can differ between tsunami and termite. Disasters do not take many forms and are not uncommon events. Disasters can affect people anywhere, any time, and can ravage people, inflict irreparable damage to the pace of their lives, and leave behind the waves of devastation and the heartbreaking scars of agony, misery and desolation. The disasters snap and tear the well-known fabric of life, which forces victims of crying and sighing lives, privation and deprivation to work significantly impaired and mutilated The government. The Govt. has been disrupted by disasters The Disaster Management Act, 2005, was passed in India. The Bill lists 'disaster' as a underlying term, "disaster," meaning a catastrophe, a disaster, a disastrous disaster or a serious occurrence in any area arising out of a natural or human cause, accident or negligence that leads to a considerable loss of life or to human damage, damage, property, damage to or damage to the environment, or to its magnetic nature or magnitude; Disasters may be the form in which the start occurs slowly as famines or as quick as earthquakes, inundation, etc. disasters. Weather disasters are natural, including flood, hurricane, blizzard, storms, earthquakes, extreme heat or cold, volcanic eruption, tsunamis. natural disasters include weather.

Human or man-made disasters include robbery, criminal damage, fire, war and terror, construction crash, accidents in transportation, industrial disasters and other technological disasters such as power cuts, gas leaks, computer network breakdown, communication failure, failure of cooling / heating / ventilation system, etc.

3.3.1. Disaster in Libraries

The center of learning is libraries. They function as cultural heritage repositories. Libraries collect, store, process and organize information / knowledge collected in papers, disseminate them and distribute it. Libraries play a crucial role in the process of educating non-formal land learning, research and growth, culture, spiritual fields, leisure and leisure. To say that booksellers act as a cornerstone of the cultural and civilization building would be no exaggeration. Modern society leads to an information society where knowledge and information are the key tools of change, strength and direction of change. Libraries allow readers to share the information and wisdom which they have collected, stored and enshrined in records over many centuries, by means of their books, publications and other teaching material. Research requires access to current knowledge and data. Libraries therefore support and encourage research, which helps to develop the economy of a nation. Libraries are designed to meet users' recreational requirements. Libraries are a core of a teaching and research academic institution. They create an environment that facilitates and promotes creativity. They assist maintain the rich understanding symbolizing the progressive march of the human race from the point of primitivism to modernism and to enlightenment.

Libraries and ICOs are susceptible to all kinds of catastrophes. No library is completely free of hazards or troubles. The catastrophe in which the library remains of significance for society was described by Paul Eden and

Graham Matthews (1996), as:' any event that threatens human security and or damages, structures and collections, facilities and installations in a library, or threatens to harm them.' They also show that a catastrophe is caused by a number of natural or human variables-

- Water (e.g. burst pipes or heavy rains leading to flooding).
- Poor storage and environmental conditions (e.g. dampness leading to mould growth).
- Inadequate security leading to break-in and theft.
- Building deficiencies-poorly maintained buildings.

Books, publications, reports, conference proceedings, rare materials and antiquities, machinery (computer, photocopying), furniture are all stocked in the library, all of which are vulnerable to catastrophe and are also component of the construction. Libraries are the core of scholarship and have data collection sources in a range of formats that need disaster-protection through catastrophe planning. Bibliothecs have modernized and automated their activities and services in this fresh technology age. Libraries use new technologies, formats and content to better fulfill the mandates for the delivery of services. New risk to library activities and obstacles to recovery of critical services following a significant disruption will accompany changes. Libraries protect human intellectual products both concrete and intangible. However, these data repositories are conducive to a natural deterioration process. Natural deterioration causes include paper acidity, copper miniature corrosion, chemical leather burning, infestation of pests, termite etc. Libraries face a Computer Virus threat as well.

In addition to this unavoidable cause of deterioration, natural hazards such as theft, vandalism, mutilation, war, terrorism, neglect and other disasters are putting libraries on the verge of high danger, for example, in wildlife, floods, turmoiles, volcanoes. These disasters have posed a serious risk to growth profits. Horrendous natural and man-made disasters in recent years which have led to the degenerative and destructive effects of very well-equipped libraries have strengthened the need for books to prepare themselves properly to deal with disasters to minimize the losses that result from such a devastating catastrophe. In preserving and making data available to libraries and data centers, libraries should also play a crucial role in ensuring their collection and accessibility. Libraries should take appropriate action to avoid disaster eruption. By carefully elaborated disaster planning, hazards or disasters in libraries can be reduced or entirely prevented. Disaster management activities to prevent the occurrence of the disaster. For instance, fires can completely enclose a library and leave no trace. So a disaster plan is vital for libraries to recognize risk factors in their fields and to draw up an unforeseen eventuality disaster plan.

3.3.2. Disaster Planning

Disaster management includes disaster management operations. disaster management. It involves the planning of disaster control, risk evaluation, training and financing needed to implement it successfully.

"A paper describing the processes designed to avoid and prepare disasters, and those that are suggested to react to and rehabilitate from disasters as they happen," according to Lyall, 1995, "the' Disaster Plan.' Different personnel members who constitute' the catastrophe team' are responsible for carrying out these duties.' The objective of a good catastrophe plan is to avoid future disasters, minimize their effect, increase their capacity to effectively and efficiently avoid, prepare and respond to disasters and build trust among stakeholders.

Disaster management should be considered an important area for the management of libraries. Core tools for disaster management should be handled by Library employees. The employees of the Library should regularly be educated in the fight against disasters. Normally the disaster plan comprises four phases

- Prevention
- Preparedness
- Reaction
- Recovery

A blue print for action should be a disaster management plan, and preparedness with all aspects should involve learning more. The employees should be educated and be conscious of the contents of the disaster plan and be separately and teamly conscious of their positions. In order to cope with any unforeseen ominous event, properly maintained equipment and material shops should be retained. Reaction phase includes that employees should understand how the alarm is raised, who they are to call in, how the material can be identified and how the undamaged material is protected. The phase of recovery includes such activities as insurance evaluation, material handling, providing consultancy, temporary service and storage and normal operation services.

The disaster control plan should be a concise and frequently reviewed and updated document for ease of use. Conservator, internal consulting officers or disaster recovery businesses are required to seek expert advice, for example. Digital materials and computing facilities should be given particular attention. The Effective Disaster Plan should be based on risk evaluation and risk management. In and outside the library, potential hazards, risks and threats should be recognized, prioritized actions relating to them and policies established to remove them or to address them to minimize their effect. Disaster control plans and primary service continuity plans should be created. These should not stop or interfere with service delivery. Alternative arrangements to provide temporary service should be made in order to minimize negative impact on business plans and revenue generation of the institution. Thapar University lost more than 70% of its collection, while the losses of Punjabi University were less than minor (T. Kaur, 2009, in two university libraries in Punjab (Patiala) India, which had been confronted with the fury of the floods in July 1993. In particular for higher education institutions in India, the author affirmed an effective disaster management Plan.

3.3.3. Disaster Management of Libraries - Disaster Management Procedures

Evaluate the harm : According to the National Task Force for Heritage Emergency (www.heritageemergency. org), a coalition of 41 domestic organisations and federal authorities, they may still be saved if books and other materials are fully soaked unless they are polluted with wastewater or chemicals.

- Is there only one region of harm, or is there damage to the entire structure?
- What was influenced by the office?
- How damaged were the materials?
- Is it easy to replace damaged goods or is it irreplaceable?
- Can they be rescued by an internal attempt or is external assistance necessary?
- Document harm through a written description and photos.
- Contacts with the sources of supply and services should be created at this moment.

Environmental stabilization : In order to avoid mold growth, the environment must be stabilized. 65 degrees and 50% moisture are the ideal conditions for a retrieval procedure.

Working with the property owner:

1. In case of power failure, portable generators.
2. Pumps for removing big amounts of standing water (which is likely not a problem on the third floor). Caution as steady water may disguise dangers.
3. Fans, especially in the damaged region, for air circulation. Fans should expel moist air from the site preferably. The national task force for Heritage Emergency advises mild indoor, if possible, air drying. It discourages the application of hair dryers, iron, ovens and long sunlight exposures.
4. Temperature and moisture measurement units P.E.M. Thermometers.
5. Dehumidifiers that reduce moisture (needs to constantly monitor temperature and moisture). Mold can form in two days, as already stated.
6. Remove products which have been harmed; stabilize atmosphere and clean area carefully. Scrub all furniture and machinery, with soap and the floors and ceilings of fungicide. Mold quickly grows and padds under tapestry. Smoke odor and fog with fungicides or insecticides should only be removed by experts.
7. "Separated damp materials: the contents are removed from drawers; pictures from damp albums; paintings and prints are removed from frameworks; towels are placed between pages of moist books"
8. "Softly clean. Loosen dirt and debris with smooth brushes and clothes on fragile objects. Avoid rubbing that could smear in dirt."
9. "Wild pictures. Clean pictures by thoroughly rinsing them into clean water. Photos of aerobics on or hanging them with plastic clothespins on plastic screens or on a paper towel. Do not let the picture get into touch when it dries with other surfaces."

10. "The damp objects and objects which are not handled should be put into open, unsealed cases or bags immediately. If you can't get them dry up in 48 hours, photos, documents, books and textiles should be frozen."

Salvage Priorities

Criteria such as

- Could items be substituted for the priorities?
- How much does it cost?
- Is the product more or less expensive than reconstruction?
- What is the product essential?
- Is it special? Is it special?

95% of all catastrophe harm is due to water, according to Illinois State University. The first choice is whether to air dry products or freeze them. Their instructions are at http:/cool.conservation-u.org/bytopic/disaster/plan/isudis.html for managing water-damaged and also fire-damaged book and non-printed materials.

Unsalvageable Materials

Materials soaked, burned, contaminated or otherwise damaged after repair must be removed. Materials which are removed after repair must be removed. For the purpose of searching for availability, replacement or withdrop for books (including removal from OCLC in the case of cataloged articles), it will be necessary to write the title pages or other available identifiers.

Pandemic Influenza

A clean, developed and well-managed library is supported by local, state and federal influenza and other outbreaks guidelines. A resource shows links to the region, government and federal plans. In emergency library bodies will endeavor to disseminate important data through its webpage and social media outlets, such as Facebook and Twitter, to the library society and beyond.

Emergency Telephone Numbers

Fire or life threatening emergency (State Emergency response numbers)

The following individuals should be contacted in the event of any type of disaster:

Landlord	xxx-xxx-xxxx
Building Supervisor/Maintenance	xxx-xxx-xxxx (cell)
Director	xxx-xxx-xxxx (home)
	xxx-xxx-xxxx (cell)
Service Center Manager	xxx-xxx-xxxx (home)
	xxx-xxx-xxxx (cell)
Fiscal Services Manager	xxx-xxx-xxxx

If the disasters prevent employees from approaching the office, then the website will be updated remotely, depending on the nature of the catastrophe, to inform membership and maybe the community.

Evacuation Procedures

RACE:	**R**escue	ensure that everyone is out of the office suite. At the same time (preferably one person does this while another staff is rescuing)—
	Alarm	pull alarm; call Emergency
	Control	if possible, use ABC fire extinguisher
	Evacuate	get out via the stairs or fire escape

Fire : Take Stairs and take Stairs.

Tornado : Take the basement stairs; the safest place underneath the staircase.

Earthquake : The most safe door jams. Do not try to leave unlike the faith of the people.

Preliminary Control Procedures from Top Universities

1. The Emergency Phone Numbers list follow processes.
2. Go out of the region for individuals.
3. If necessary, take measures to shut down water.
4. Protection by plastic sheets or other suitable means of endangered fields.
5. Water dripping in buckets, garbage cans and so on.
6. Water drainage monitoring area from fresh fields. If accessible, check also floors above and below and adjacent regions.
7. Take measures needed for environmental stability. The air should circulate; 65 degrees F and 50 percent RH are optimal temperature and moisture.

Avoid

- Entering an area until it is declared secure.
- Attempt to open the moist book (one tear costs one or more Dollar.
- Attempt to close open books which are swollen.
- Utilizing the mechanical presses on moist material.
- Tentative of distinct books stuck together.
- Bleaches, detergents, water soluble fungicides.
- The use of any type of colored paper during rescue and restoration.
- In boxes, pack newly-dry products or leave them for more than two days unattended.
- Saturated materials are placed next to the materials that are slightly harmed.
- Removal of book or scoring covers.

Emergency Equipment & Supplies To Have Readily

- Batteries (flashlight)
- Boxes (flat)
- Bricks

- Brooms
- Buckets
- Chemical sponges
- Crates
- Dehumidifiers
- Drying racks
- Drying space
- Extension cords
- Fans
- First aid kits
- Flashlights
- Freezer facilities
- Freezer paper
- Fungicides
- Generators, portable
- Hair Dryer
- Masks
- Mops
- Paper towels
- Plastic clothes pins
- Plastic sheeting
- Plastic trash bags
- Rubber gloves
- Scales
- Sponges
- String (study)
- Thermometers
- Transistor radio

Conclusion

Libraries should pursue a disaster management plan effectively. The plan must be tracked and checked on a regular basis. Periodic mocking of the complete scale should be performed. The buildings, facilities, collections and computers of the library should be fully insured. Good drainage and flood-resistant system should be available. It should be constructed to seismically secure library buildings. Regular controls on water leakage should be undertaken in the library building. Library and resources building should be maintained correctly and periodic building and equipment inspections should be carried out. In the event of an emergency, fire extinguishers should be inspected and employees should be trained to handle the devices. The structure of the library building should make it possible to prevent precious reading material from the ground floor which could be lost in floods, especially if the region is vulnerable to flooding. In the library building, basement should be prevented. Single switch control should be mounted and electrical installations should be equipped in a safe mode. Properly shelved and cleaned stacks should be provided. Termitis therapy in the library should be performed on a regular basis. The library should be intended to minimize possible losses in the event of an earthquake. Not only to inspect the facilities but to train library employees, Mock exercises should be conducted periodically. Human safety should be the first priority in the event of a disaster. A list of all disaster team members should be included and their responsibilities clearly set out throughout disaster phases should be provided in the disaster control plan. It should also be specified how often this task needs to be performed. Committed and devoted employees are needed to coordinate and succeed in the actions of the catastrophe plan. The digitization of valuable cultural and heritage resources is a significant means of conservation. It's essential to have digital archiving. Archiving documents involves standards and formats that never deteriorate and are often an active migration process. The basis for digital resource archiving and the validation of digital documents are metadata standards, including EAD (encoding archive) description, for discovering guidelines and EACs(encoding archive material).

Disaster management plan is not only essential but also crucial. Disaster management plan for disasters. Required disaster management infrastructure should be established and an emergency reaction mechanism established and upgraded if necessary. It is essential and immensely important to educate and build people's knowledge about disaster management. Various library kinds should work together and the national library should play the leading role in the development of a disaster planning model. Libraries can share or pool their institutions for disaster rescue. Catastrophe Management Library collaboration can be followed in various ways such as joint training programmes, procurement and storage of emergency materials, etc. Governmental institutions and professional organizations should also provide information and training for libraries and library professionals in disaster management.

3.4. CARE AND HANDLING OF LIBRARY RESOURCES

Introduction

What are the main threats to library material?

- The nature of the material itself
- Natural and man-made disasters
- The environment in which it is kept
- The way material is handled

A broad variety of organic products, including paper, cloth, animal skin and adhesive, are included in traditional library collections. The method of natural ageing of such organic compounds is continuous and unavoidable. While measures to slow this deterioration can be taken with careful treatment and a supportive environment, it can not be stopped completely. The chemical and physical stability of the library material also relies on the quality and handling, together with the design and construction of the final object, of raw goods used in their manufactures.

Over the decades, mass manufacturing pressures have decreased material quality in libraries. A large proportion of the paper stock produced after 1850 is extremely acidic, breaks and destroys themselves in time. For automation purposes, binding methods are shortened and many text blocks are now only kept together by adhesive. Indeed, all books and especially leather bindings are much more damage-prone than most people value. Modern media such as microforms, visual and optical disks, digital formats, pictures, audio and visual media are all subject to intrinsic conservation issues and must be properly stored and used if not lost early.

It is generally hard to recognize that a big quantity of library material reaches the end of its natural lives and can only be extended by careful storage and handling for the few years remaining.

Why preserve?

- The library sort and the way it is used represent its collections' need for conservation. Obviously, the conditions of conservation of a local public lending library differ from those of a national library. However, for a few years or for forever, both are required to maintain and maintain their collection available.
- Libraries cannot afford economically to allow premature wear out of their holdings. It is costly, even if possible, to substitute library material. Maintenance is economically sound.
- What will interest researchers in the future can not be readily anticipated. The best way to serve future users is to preserve current collections.
- Leading and professional library employees should

devote themselves to the care and maintenance of the material they work with.

Who is responsible?

Everybody's accountable. While conservation specialists can advise and undertake specific activities, it is the responsibility of all the library employees, from the bottom up to the bench, to protect the welfare of their holdings. Preservation measures must be supported and encouraged from the uppermost to the youngest levels in the library.

The managers who manage the library and maintain the external and internal structures of the building must have close contact with the collectors. For instance, if money is spent to redirect and replace a building's lighting, the opportunity should be used not only to ensure energy-saving lighting but also to fulfill certain lighting criteria. All the stakeholders should ensure that the risk to collections is decreased and not increased by piping running through regions in which library material is available when plumbing is installed or substituted. Clear communication is the key in these cases.

The library's conservation demands need to be taken into account in accordance with the social and political environment in which it works. It is also necessary to take into consideration the objective of the organization, the collection of policies and accessible resources. Considering the reasons, in consultation with multiple agencies, conservation strategies must therefore be adopted for the following reasons:

- Additional copies of heavily-use material, such as reference works, should be ready for purchases and collection when the price to repair such articles is higher than the price to replace them. It is also important that the cost and efficiency of supplemental copies (i.e. microform or digital versions and readership machines) are more cost-effective and efficient than hard copy access.

- Policies to guide customers to substitute substitutes rather than originals and the most suitable copy should be agreed in conjunction with cataloging and records creation operations in the library.
- Departments should schedule good enough acquisition housing.
- Room readers should be kept informed of all restrictions on the use, and briefed on photocopy constraints.
- Resources should be provided for training staff on security for themselves and for library material, on how to handle library material correctly, and on how best to pass this knowledge on to users.
- An exhibition policy should be drawn up which ensures that items will not come to harm while on exhibition, whether within the library or on loan to other institutions. Librarians and conservation staff should agree on whether items are fit for display. Adequate support and security, and suitable environmental conditions for material to be exhibited, should be enforced.
- Preservation staff and those responsible for the collections, whatever their level of experience, should not only have some technical and scientific knowledge, but should also be familiar with the history of collections, the material they are made of, and the contents of the documents –so as to be able to understand better the preservation problems. Librarians, library staff at all levels, and students of librarianship should be acquainted with the importance of preservation within a library's overall function and policy.

Where to begin?

Part of the process of formulating a preservation

policy is to define whether, and to what extent, the library will acquire and retain material. There can be no general guidance for libraries on what material should be selected for acquisition and future preservation; this will depend on each individual library and its policy.

However, national and regional libraries should cooperate in sharing the responsibilities of what to preserve and retain.

In order to be able to care for its holdings, a library must make a comprehensive and honest assessment of the physical state of the institution, the collections, and their preservation requirements. Moreover, to care for collections with a limited budget and limited resources, it is important that decisions are made on a clear and rational basis. Such an assessment can be done internally, by the library itself, or by independent consultants, whose expertise is established –both have advantages and disadvantages. Consultants are expensive and take up a lot of staff time. However, the final assessment should reveal the stark truth of the facts. An internal assessment will probably be cheaper but might be influenced by staff politics. Unfortunately, it is also usually easier to accept recommendations from a body outside than from within.

Such an undertaking must be a cooperative effort of all the departments and be endorsed at the most senior level. An assessment without authority is likely to be ineffectual. The final report is obviously critical to the success of any 'needs' survey. It should clearly identify the risks to the collections and be realistic in its proposals.

How to begin?

It is important to have a clear idea of the objectives of the study before investigations into the state of the institution and its collections begin. Details on policies, operations and procedures may be found in written documents, the most likely sources will be through interviews with library staff at all levels, observations on how material is cared for and handled by staff and users, and risk assessments on the buildings and collections.

Identifying major and immediate threats to the library's holdings or particular collections should be of primary concern. Such threats will vary for different institutions, from renewing a fire and smoke detection system, through setting up an integrated pest management programme, to moving an important collection of photographs to an area with a more stable environment.

Surveys are a fundamental tool for developing a library's preservation policy. However, while they should be comprehensive, they do not necessarily have to be too detailed. Surveys can often result in enormous amounts of information being accumulated which later become very difficult to put into order and analyze. Short questions and answers are the key to successful surveys. The purposes of four surveys which will help to form the basis of the assessment are summarized below. The ensuing chapters will provide more ideas on what to look out for when planning the surveys.

Building : to define any threats to safety or the environment posed by the institution's site; define the building's history and use and determine its external and inner fabric status.

Prevention and reaction to the disasters : to identify prospective risk to structures and collections, whether man-made or naturally occurring; to review precautions against these hazards; and to examine the preparedness and reaction plans for disasters.

Environment : report on the environmental measures in place to preserve collections; what are the good and bad points and who is liable.

Collection : to identify prospective issues and assess the present situation of the collection. Description of the type and quantity of items in the collection will contribute to an overview of the stock of the library (e.g. 300 pictures, 2,000 books or "linear" meters of boxes) and the age (e.g. 10,000 books before 1850; 20,000 books between 1850 and 1900, and 500,000 books between 1900 and present). Additional points to cover include:

- What is the collections' overall condition?
- Which collections are especially poor?
- What are the most valuable / important collections?
- What are the most at risk collections?
- How quickly do the collections grow?
- What is the probable direction to take for collecting?
- Are there room for future collections accessible or space assigned?

Knowing which material is widely used will contribute to the identification of the conservation requirements of certain collections. For instance, a frequently demanded and in bad conditions number of local historical publications can become a greater concern on microfilming than any newspapers that are not often used, but are also in bad condition.

Other areas which will be highlighted in future chapters, such as collection safety, storage and handling of materials, the condition of storage fields, reading room practice and personnel preparation and knowledge, must be recorded too.

What should be maintained?

The next step is to prioritize the recommendations that have been made when an assessment of preservation needs has been conducted. In order to decide what to do in order to

- secure the building fabric
- improve environmental control
- improve collections storage and handling, both because of the restricted funds and the prospective

extent of the issue, it is essential to be selective.

Such selectivity must be an explicit part of a library policy if it is to properly fulfill its responsibilities towards future users. It should be understood that the holistic approach to care for library collections does not preclude selectiveness. Every library material should be protected from disasters caused by human beings, theft and mutilation, pest and mould attacks and bad management practices not for special attention in the manner in which they are used or kept in certain environmental conditions.

In general it is common sense to choose materials for specific preservation processes like reformatting or boxing. Boxing a goodly collection that is not used until a poorly-formed and heavily-used collection is not reasonable, nor does reformatting the material that an organization otherwise has redesigned.

What are the consequences for the economy?

The quantity of data contained in libraries is nearly always higher than the resources to achieve its goals. Everything can't and never have been saved. An indefinite or permanent retention commitment includes significant economic spending on lodging, unique storage circumstances and, potentially, reformatting. Decisions must therefore be taken regarding what is collected and preserved.

Each library has an obligation to protect current and future customers in its collections. The fact that maintaining and retaining collections costs cash is not avoided. Libraries spend too long on acquisitions to a large extent in their budget. Most libraries have insufficient or insufficient funds allocated to preservation. It is almost always cheaper than repairing or replacing it to spend time and resources to prevent damage to library material.

No library can allow any precautionary action to take against fire, flood, robbery and infestation with moulds or insects; it is highly costly in terms of human and economic resources to recover materials suffering from these disasters. These disruptions have multiple consequences. Serious disasters are often triggered by conditions that could at little price be prevented. Not only is prevention better than treatment, but it is more often cheaper.

The provision of library equipment does not necessarily mean excessive library fund expenditure. The issues of conservation are often common sense and cost-effective. All libraries should, though, realize that it is so important to preserve and maintain their collections as to buy them and that adequate funds should be allocated accordingly.

Why and whom do you collaborate?

It is not enough for librarians to be conscious of their responsibility to preserve their collections, although the first necessity is knowledge. It is also essential that the public and those able to finance conservation programs become more aware of this. Governments should play an active part in the welfare of the heritage of a nation. If a country's written heritage is to survive in any format, national preservation agencies, financially supported both by government and private funding, are essential. These establishments should be able to encourage the adoption of sound policies by all libraries and institutions. Very helpful services are not enough, such as providing catastrophe scheduling literature, photocopying or safety questions on demand. There should also be active training and training.

In addition, national conservation offices may sometimes be suitable national coordination bodies for retention policies. They may also be a political mouthpiece for libraries on matters such as compulsory publication usage of permanent paper. Another useful responsibility that national conservation agencies can take up is to educate the general public through poster campaigns in schools and libraries on the respect and attention of library material.

To survive as a nation's heritage, domestic, regional, consortium and institutional programs must be co-ordinated. It is not realistic to hope that libraries and archives solve the technical and economic conservation issues at domestic level separately and successfully. In 1996, for example, in order to raise awareness on conservation issues and to co-ordinate activities in the region, the IFLA and ICA created the Joint IFLA-ICA Committee on Conservation in Africa (JIPTA).

Not only archives, but also museum and gallery should cooperate with libraries. Substantial savings and effort duplication can be avoided in fields such as environmental control, construction and collection evaluation, and disaster preparedness and reconstruction plans by institutions that consult each other.

3.4.1. Security

The library manager is responsible for initiating, coordinating and implementing a library safety policy. Other libraries, police and personnel should be consulted when drawing up such a policy.

3.4.1.1. Securing perimeters and buildings

- Perimeters and terrains of the library should be kept clean.
- The facility of access for criminals should be evaluated in building outdoors. Serious account should be given to an alarm and a closed-circuit TV system. It should be well lit in all areas.
- In terms of locks, safety glass or film, close attention should be paid to the windows and the doors.
- The construction interior should be kept clean. It presents an image of care and surveillance that deters possible criminals.

- If necessary, separate and staffed all entry / exit points or routes.

When not in use, all personnel areas should be closed.

- Costly equipment must be chained or bolted down with markings of safety.

Sign in or out of the library and always wear passes should be signed by all contractors.

- The staff should be encouraged to have an alert attitude.
- Secure and clear policy guidance on who has access to which areas should be maintained in all storage fields.
- The safety of rare / valuable material should be addressed through specific measures, such as the use of vaults.

Preventional measures for damaging of Library materials : Today, college libraries face a challenging scenario because, in spite of restricted budgets and uncertainties, they are anticipated to enhance their output. Decision manufacturers can use the fast development of electronic materials and the decrease of printing material to restrict the distribution of resources for the physical library buildings. University Libraries are therefore challenged to show the effect on the community they serve of their premises. Therefore, the significance of an academic library in its location and the use of space are very important.

The core of the campus and the most important government teaching space of the university have always been library buildings. Today, while library resources are increasingly used by scientists in their offices through a network, university libraries are a workshop of learners and a meeting and studying area.

The significance of a contemporary and well-equipped campus library building is underlined. In addition, college libraries function as an e-learning gateway requiring local access to a networked setting and functional computers.

Monitoring : There was also monitoring to see how the library as a room and as a location is used and important. Safety of users is the ultimate objective of all the growth of the University Library of Tampere. It is thought that helpful proof has been gathered concerning the day-to-day use of library facilities and that in the future this data will benefit the library. It is also gratifying that the library in Tampere has become a location and a place for customer satisfaction.

Library Safety Related to Space and Design

The planning of new library structures and the refurbishment of the ancient structures became difficult at the start of the 21st century. Historically, the main buildings for the library were housed and study and research were conducted. Libraries are now confronted with a paradigm shift in their understanding of how and how library installations operate (Cantor and Schomberg 2003; Boone 2003).

Boone (2003) defines the move from the traditional library design as material storage centres to new installations with multiple functions, more complicated, improved, interactive and research-support environments.

The college library as a location is a teaching and learning resource centre that is used as a workroom for learners. Changes in higher education, such as the participation of e-learning and the library and the pedagogical change in higher education, make the education more a process of co-operation between professors and students which influence the use of library spaces. The library is often designed to play a greater role in education and study, with schools, meeting rooms and computer laboratories, all of which are component of the library in terms of room and place (Leighton and Weber, 1999). The functions of libraries have been altered and services offered by technology.

Changes in electronic resources supply and fresh digital facilities are affecting the planning of libraries, as demand for (to shop) room in many libraries is declining.

Together with library stakeholders, faculty members and students, the approach has been drawn up and is essential to the library's growth. This vision makes it clear that the library is able to obtain proof of the daily use of the library, the proof-based development of library facilities, including library buildings, and to provide librarians with the ability to provide services to satisfy library customer requirements.

The University Library as a site is also a government space that improves social capital. Social capital can be described as people's capacity to work together in communities and organisations for common reasons (Gloziene 2005). Johnson and Griffis (2009) describe the advantage of preserving and/or extending one's social ties and interactions, and describe that social capital. They stress the significance of social capital investigation as a way to understand the nature of library use. They discovered a powerful connection among the social capital indices and the library use in their research of public libraries. As a location, there are more than just government and academic libraries, collections and individuals. They are a place where ideas and messages are collected and shared and social capital improved (Crawford 1999). Given that university libraries in Finland have a large part to play in improving social capital, not only for the scholarly community but also for the general public.

The library clearly receives helpful data for the planning of facilities and hours of service from outcomes such as this. Nevertheless, a study should take into account the danger of generalizing too broadly, as well as likely trends and changes in customer utilization patterns. However, further research is necessary. Continuous modifications in the customers ' usage habits on library sites should be followed regularly to guarantee that the building is designed with the safest possible means.

The surveys have revealed relevant spatial planning data.

A plan that answers these findings will be implemented by the library. For example, the survey and monitoring results from 2010 have shown that peaceful workplaces are needed in the library. This should be taken seriously by the library and ensure that these demands are resolved in a quieter place. It may even have to adjust current equipment in order to provide quieter space / areas. Hopefully, as comparatively fresh major changes will not be necessary in the premises.

According to researches, it is evident that learners use computers from the library, so the accessibility of computer workplaces and a number of pcs is an issue for the library, even though clients now use their own laptops progressively in the library. The library therefore assured that there were desks without pcs but that they were supplied with electrical sockets for pcs in addition to a wireless network.

Physical Hazards in Libraries

The studies show that the students use library computers, so computer workplace accessibility and some computers are a problem for the library although customers are now increasingly using their own laptops in the library. Therefore, the library guarantees that there are desks without computers, but in relation to the wireless network, they have electric sockets for computers.

If library privileges must be suspended for the purpose of protecting library collections, equipment or other people, the Library employees shall directly notify the suspension upon occurrence. The suspension of access to the equipment and borrowing rights shall be deemed temporary and restored if the client suspended shows remediation of the originating scenario. This may include evidence of skilled exterminations at the main customer residence, evidence of medical attention, or additional evidence to satisfy the conditions if necessary. This may also be necessary. Copies of receipts for therapy may be included, a letter from a licensed pest control business or a written declaration from the proprietor or manager of a multi-family home may contain confirmatory data. Proof of a change of address may also be recognized in certain conditions.

Returning Material that may be brought in touch with pests The client SHOULD NOT return the material through a book drop if the library products come into touch with bed bugs, roaches, lice, flushes or other insects or plagues while in the ownership of the client. Place the products instead in a safely locked plastic bag, and instantly notify an employee when they return the products to the circulation desk, allowing the employee to take needed precautions. Input with a bed bug or other infestation will be processed or discarded at the discretion of the library. Customer may charge the material that has to be discarded at the complete replacement value and all applicable fines and fees circulation policies apply. If materials become infested, library privileges may be permanently removed.

3.4.1.2. Preventing criminal and anti-social behavior

Criminal and anti-social conduct ranges from the rude visitor to the determined thief. The risk lies with the personnel, books, equipment and personal assets.

- having a calm, ordered library
- building an atmosphere that the genuine reader considers helpful, effective, but that the villain feels anxious and careful

- having prominent information that clearly defines what is an unacceptable behavior
- training personnel in the way they treat an aggressive or uncomfortable user or suspect
- Security in the area to be read
- How are loose items issued and how are checked when they are returned?
- How well are surveillance areas read?
- are safety equipment in location?
- are bags permitted and checked on the exit in these areas?

3.4.1.3. Security of library material

Every library material should be stamped so that it is clear that it belongs to a given institution. Library stamps should be quick-drying, stable, and unfading. If available, safety marking systems should be checked frequently.

Emergency information brochure Useful for all staff in case of:

- staff accidents and visits
- Vandalism, stealing and attacks
- incidents such as power failure, power lift failure, safety key losses
- Emergencies threatening the welfare system;
- Incidental and emergency information brochure, listing just the immediate actions to be taken;
- hurricane, earthquake, and flood warnings.

3.4.2. Disaster Planning

Any library, regardless of size, should take every possible precaution to prevent a disaster which can be avoided. Measures to tackle the consequences of disasters, be they natural or man-made, are equally important.

Natural	Man Made
Hurricanes	Acts of war and terrorism
Floods	Fires
Earthquakes	Water (broken pipes, leaking roofs, etc.)
Volcanic eruptions	Explosions
Sandstorms	

Numerous resources have been published to aid institutions in implementing disaster avoidance measures and formulating a disaster response and salvage plan. Only the key points are listed here. A written plan in which all those elements are fully developed should be required for each library.

In disaster prevention (as is generally possible in conservation operations), a' phased' method can be used. In the first stage, it is therefore acceptable to commence with some sections, even in the overview form, especially if the institution concentrates primarily on the most relevant issues. In a later phase, the planners can gradually add more details and additional sections to enhance the education, time to pursue the plan and consensus as to how the institution should organize its preparatory work.

Disaster measures usually involve five phases

Risk assessment	ascertaining the dangers to the building and its collections
Prevention	implementing measures which will remove or reduce any danger
Preparedness	developing a written preparedness, response, and recovery plan
Response	procedures to follow when disaster strikes
Recovery	restoring the disaster site and damaged material to a stable and usable condition.

Risk assessment

Try to define any external and internal threats that could cause collection issues and to evaluate any deficiencies in the existing catastrophe prevention policies. Consultation with fire departments helps to identify potential risks that are not immediately apparent.

Describe the area in which collections are stored (residential, industrial, shopping center, rural, leisure)

3.4.2.1. Identifying external environmental threats

- Is it nearby to the collection site (airport, road / motorway and natural waterway, such as the ocean, lakes, rivers, natural or buzzing grounds, other buildings), that there are significant industrial or natural hazards?
- In what immediate surroundings (fence and gateway, natural obstacles such as rivers, lakes, ocean front, dark corners, overhangs, areas with a cover) or perimeter to a building?
- Are the environments secure (controlled routine patrols, efficient lights, secure doors, controlled access, individual access to visitors and staff)?
- Are factories, traffic or environmental pollution (dust, gas pollutants) a problem?
- How safety is fire and flood building–are natural hazards, such as forests and the river or the petrochemical ones, present in the area?
- Durable incidents or disasters (bombing and bombing, civil unrest, riots, wars, natural disasters–floods, earthquakes, fire, dust storm, vandalism) have taken place in the last 5 years?

3.4.2.2. Identifying internal environmental threats

- Which materials are used in the building structure?
- Is fire-resistant to the external and internal construction tissue?

- Are there fireproof walls separating building components and fireproof doors?
- Are the water pipes, heaters, air conditioning, kitchen and the lab stored in collections at a safe distance from the plumbo, electrical and mechanical installations?
- Is the area in which leak-proof or flood-proof collections are stored?
- Is there any area that allows smoking?
- Are there large amounts (such as chemicals in laboratories) of flammable material other than the on site books?

3.4.2.3. Assessing current preventive measures

- Does the construction have a smoke, fire or water detection system?
- Is the fire extinguishing system automatically available in the area?
- What kind are there in the region (extinguishers-water, foam, CO2, fire hoses...) of manual firefighting devices?
- Are regular inspection systems for fire detection and/ or extinguishing?
- Do lightning conductors exist in the building?
- Are special precautions taken where dangerous activities such as the rewire and renovation of the building's inner and outer fabric are being carried out?
- Is the building safety system (if any) linked to the department of fire / police?
- Does the library have a written plan for preparing and responding to disasters?
- *Elements*: descriptions of the urgent processes; outline of disaster reaction; list of emergencies; priorities for recovery; conservation specialists, off-

site storage of supplies; list of personnel volunteers; other elements.

- Are personnel trained in emergency intervention procedures (delegated officers, ongoing training, and evacuations)?
- Data backed up by the computer every day?
- Is there a duplicate and off-site stored manual access to catalogues, registration and accession records?
- Is it duplicated and stored off-site electronic catalog and documents?

3.4.2.4. Prevention

Take all the precautions needed to safeguard library buildings and their holdings after the risk has been evaluated. Emergency services (fire, police and hospital) are consulted.

3.4.2.4.1. Fire alarm systems

The fire and smoke detection system should be installed in all parts of the building, alerting occupants and the local Fire Brigade simultaneously. Early warning of a developing fire can be provided by smoke detectors, which allows manual deletion before a sprinkler system activation. There should also be manually operated fire-alarm calling points, which occupants can use to indicate the presence of fire or smoke.

- Slip boards or shelving racks to ensure that all components of the building are within 6 meters of the bucket of a fully extended pit, should be installed if an automatic fire removing system is not available.
- Hydrant systems or raised handrails on all structures over 30 m high or over 1000 m^2 of a single floor.
- The hydrant or increasing mains should be situated in order to allow the piping from outside the building by the fire brigade to pressurize.

- Portable fire extinguishers should always be available, even if an automatic fire suppression system has been installed. There should be a suitable number of hand-held extinguishers (CO, , water, or foam according to the likely cause of fire, i.e., electrical or chemical) strategically placed.

3.4.2.4.2. Automatic extinguishing systems

The benefits of an automatic fire extinction system should be taken into consideration.

- Only a CO2 gas system is appropriate for larger compartments, i.e. areas that are not usually occupied by individuals and that can be rendered airtight.
- Halon gas systems are no longer manufactured because they are harmful to the environment, especially to the ozone protective layer of the ground.
- Wet tubes are a reliable, secure and comparatively easy-to-maintain technique of extinguishing. The activation of the sprinkler does not cause all sprinklers to function, contrary to popular belief, and thus the risk of accidental discharge is not to be overestimated. The average sprinkler releases between 15 and 20 liters per minute, while the typical fire pants emit between 540 and 1125 liters per minute (120 and 250 gallons per minute). It should be remembered that, contrary to the possible impact of various chemical agents, the environmental and human safety aspects of water are known. In addition, recuperation techniques are known for water-damaged materials.
- Dry tube sprinkler systems are essentially the same as wet tube systems except that the tube containing pressurized air in the protected area. The valve opens when the sprinkler is activated so that water flows through the roofs. This reduces the risk of leaking water into collecting regions.

- We have developed micromist systems that release small quantities of water at very high pressures resulting in extraordinarily efficient cooling and fire control at very low water levels. Tests have been demonstrated to prevent water saturation, often linked to standard firefighting procedures. Additional advantages are expected: reduced installation costs, minimal esthetic effect, and recognized environmental security.

3.4.2.4.3. Routine maintenance

The maintenance and routine testing shall be conducted of fire alarms and removal systems, building fabric, plumbing, gas and electric supplies and fittings, etc. All reports and any maintenance work should be maintained and documented.

- Plan floor plans indicating storage areas, windows, accesses and exits, extinguishers for the fire, fire warning, sprinklers, smoke-fire-sensors, water, gas and heating piping, lifts controls, electrical and water supply and stop-points are required.

3.4.2.4.4.1. PREPAREDNESS

The following are to be regularly prepared, revised and updated:

- Priority rescue lists by departments which specify which items should be recovered from each room. The fire services can provide entry for a short period of time to a building for rescue purposes and it should be known which items should be stored and where.
- The emergency intervention team consisting of voluntary staff living near the library will be selected and training. The team should be proven to remove the material and take choices about rescue methods confidently. It is vital that they participate in disaster workshops that simulate a disaster site and practice methods.

Detailed step by step guidance on all phases of recovery, covering a variety of events (e.g. dome / plumber leaks, floods, and fires) and the different media contained in the collections, such as books and newspapers, manuscripts / records, coated vs. uncoated inventory, sound recordings, photographic media, computer / electronic media, etc.

- Areas for the registration and packing of material.
- Places for temporary staff and material rehousing.
- Local freezer contracts.
- Vacuum drying contracts.
- Transport services arrangements.
- Transportation, cleaning and sortation equipment supplies.
- Forms of registration: various copies of all forms required in the resource, including stock forms, packaging lists, requests and purchases, etc.
- Information on accounting: a description and access procedures of institutional assets, accessible in retrieval attempt.
- Insurance information: coverage explanations, claims processes, recordkeeping requirements, staff / volunteer restrictions on disaster entry and state / federal disaster relief procedures.

3.4.2.4.4.2. RESPONSE

- Follow the emergency procedures established to elevate the alarm, evacuate personnel and secure the disaster site.
- The catastrophe reaction team leader should be contacted and the emergency reaction team should be brief and led.
- If authorization is granted for re-enter the site the damage, equipment and supplies, and services required shall be preliminarily assessed.

- Adjust the environment to prevent growth of mold, if necessary.
- Photograph of material damaged for the purposes of insurance claims.
- Establish a recording and packaging zone requiring freezing and a mildly moist air-drying zone, and other minor treatments.
- Carriage to the closest freezing plant of water-damaged products.

3.4.2.4.5. Drying of moist material

It is vital to be acquainted with distinct methods of drying distinct kinds of library material as part of the preparing of a disaster plan. Air drying • Drying • Freeze drying • Vacuum thermal drying • Freeze drying When it is necessary to decide critically, books and records should be frozen in order to reduce physical distortion and biological contamination. The following methods are of advantage and advantage to dry.

3.4.2.4.5.1. AIR-DRYING

The simplest way of drying the damp, not totally wet, material is by air-drying. On its end, a moist book can be stood and its pages can be blown away or interwoven with blotting paper. Although this is an effective technique that does not require costly machines or materials (fans and interleaving paper), it is hard-working and time consuming.

3.4.2.4.5.1.1. RECOVERY

- Specify preservation priorities. Consultation with the conservatives on the best cleaning and repair methods. Get estimates of costs.
- Develop a phased conservation program when involving large amounts of material.
- Choose items from those justifying special treatments to be discarded, replaced or rebounded.

- The disaster site is cleaned and restored.
- Replace the material treated at the renovated site.
- Disaster analysis and experience improvements in the plan.

The availability of temporary storage facilities and other services it can provide should be connected with local and district authorities / communities. Working together with other books, museums and galleries in the region can save time, money and resources.

Fire System

Archives and libraries have precious and unique conservation documents. Wherever archives are used, fire and smoke damage can be damaged–in museums, libraries, government constructions, hospitals and sectors. This is why it is essential to ensure a high level of security in your archive and library.

Today's security solutions are adapted to the demands of your archive and library and offer maximum protection from all hazards. They offer everything from advising to commissioning and after-sales service for fiber identification and extinguishing on the basis of the idea of a skilled and innovative partner.

Fire control panels : Each fire safety solution is concentrated on the contemporary fire control panel. It transforms a fi re alarm into alarm alarms, evacuation and extinction measures. The extremely easy user interface with prompting texts allows users to rapidly monitor system status locally or remotely.

Voice alarm system : In case of a fire, the fire sensing system activates the speech alarm system automatically. It transmits clear alarms and evacuation messages in the archive or library and the nearest regions with voice announcements, to ensure evacuation before an extinguishing agent is used.

Extinguishing control panels : Fire detection and

extinction are combined with extinction control panels by acting as an interface between the two: the paired fire panels activate the extinguishing system, after getting a fire alarm from the linked detectors. They can be used for applications from one or more sectors. Further repeater terminals permit remote control of control panels for extinguishing.

Aspirating Smoke Detection

It is an extremely delicate device in ventilated archives or libraries for the earliest fire detection possible, reducing the risk of fire harm. It is generally used in the atmosphere in and outputs of an archive or library as well as in the room's detection system.

Point type fire detectors : In the archive or library zone, sophisticated fire detectors are used. The parameter sets provide unmatched safety for detection to guarantee early recognition. In archives and libraries where a smolding fire is likely to be high, this is particularly critical. This operates so well that newest fire system businesses offer a true S-LINE fire detector alarm guarantee.

H2O gas : H2O Gas provides the greatest extinguishing effectiveness on the market today for the protection of archives and libraries. It combines the excellent extinguishing performance of nitrogen with water nebula based on nitrogen and water that cools burning or heated surfaces. Even for very delicate assets, the limited water requirements make it appropriate.

Access control : The Access Control system offers secure and flexible authorisation for access, time logging and issuing of badges.

Pin codes or a fingerprint reader are suggested in a high-value archive or library.

Video surveillance : The video monitoring system controls critical zones such as the entrance region of the archive or library or government places to record occurrences prior to and after a case.

Alarm indicators : If an invisible fibre detector triggers an alarm, the alarm indicator identifies the endangered region rapidly.

Extinguishing with Nitrogen : N_2 is based on pure nitrogen and provides an extremely valid alternative for records containing assets that are waterless.

When extra pressure constraints are encountered in a protected space, fire systems give CDT N_2, a unique CDT technology to minimize the pressure and turbulence.

Intrusion detection : Unlicensed access detection. For each type of danger and application, modern innovations provide a complete variety of appliances.

RFID : Radio Frequency Identification (RFID) Asset Tracing is the system for locating valuable properties in archives and libraries in real time through the use of active RFID Wireless Tags. The location and movement of controlled assets-based scenarios provide flexible safety requirements. The RFID tags with a battery power are shielded from manipulation. They are equipped with infrared and RFID transmission and a motion detector.

General Guide for Safety in Libraries

There are a broad variety of automated and manual work for people working in libraries. These jobs can be allocated to one or several people in big libraries. The same individual may perform a number of distinct duties in smaller libraries. A number of health and safety risks are present in library job. The risks include psychological stress, slip, travel and fall risk, damage in the back, concern for personal safety, bad workplaces, illumination, powders, molds and low indoor air quality.

The following guide gives a general overview of hazard recognition, assessment and control techniques in libraries. Basic health and safety elements are described.

Fire safety in Libraries around the world : The library has an uncommon structure with big fire loads and complex functions. It can lead to losses of assets, unforeseeable losses and political effect following the fire. On 30 January 2015, the second biggest library in Moscow burst into fire. That produced around 1,000 square meter of roof crumbling; a large number of valuable ancient books and political literature were destroyed and burned on the three levels of library. In the 1980s, some developed countries systematically started studying the building technique of fire safety based on performance. Over 20 types of evacuation models and the appropriate calculation software have been created with the growth of computer technology.

Fire smoke is a buoyancy regulated air disturbance and individuals will be first subjected to smoke in high-rise structures due to air's convection impacts. If the alarm is consistent, the time required to safely evacuate depends on the amount of personal evacuation time affected, including stairs, building height, total number of people affected and the evacuation rate of single bodies modified. In the evacuation, because of the construction of joint stairs, the third, second and first exits were crowded and the employees could not be evacuated safely through the stairs, but also the evacuation time increased.

The main characteristic of each university is libraries. They stop for potential learners and relatives before they leave for the library to purchase bumper stickers and sweat shirts. For some learners, libraries are the second home, a retreat for those with noisy classrooms or those who need to alter the landscape during their studies.

Testudo, the mascot for my alma mater, is proudly situated in front of the primary library of the school, in which learners passing by can rub their noses for luck on their course. It was rumored that the GPA university pupils fell by the year when the library was closed for renovation, learners could not obtain their fortuneful Testudo fix. I wonder whether it was because of the inaccessibility of Testudo or because the library was closed. The last one had more to do with him, having the idea as a sensation.

Universal Codes for Fire Safety

The sprinkler safety requirements for sprinkler installation standards are based on a sort of hazard in a room. The greater the risk, the more water it takes to regulate a fire in the room. Lists of the kinds of fuel loads observed in light, normal and additional hazards are given in Annex A of the standard. Not only is the commodity itself determined by the level of the risk; it also concerns the arrangement of the risk.

The more the product is tightly packaged, the greater the danger. Some of the book storage fields are therefore regarded to be more dangerous than others and need more water for space protection. Additional sprinklers may be needed if obstacles to the water release are present in order to guarantee that the water is able to achieve the risk.

Library classifications are regarded lower than their stack fields or libraries. While traditional libraries often have aisles broader than 30 inches and can store only up to 8 feet, book stacking places often include smaller aisles and bigger racks up to the roof. Due to the lack of the minimum clearance of 18 inches needed by other parts of the standard in the stacking zones, particular sprinkler positioning criteria for the stacking fields of the library are given.

Compact portable shelf studies showed that the light-hazardous sprinkler could properly protect it. The configuration of the storage and area is limited to the tests that were approved but fire control was achieved in densities similar to that provided in the traditional library, including the larger coverage areas per sprinkler, with the specified transverse and longitudinal barriers.

The sprinkler system should be assessed whenever the room is reconfigured or altered. As already stated, the localizing requirements for sprinklers vary based on the configuration of the shelf storage. The system of sprinklers must be evaluated to guarantee that the new hazard is protected, both with regard to the appropriate discharge densities and to obstruction regulations.

In order to ensure effective use of the life-saving features on the building and prevent fires, the plan aims to provide all occupants with safety data in the event of a fire. This fire security plan was intended to match Chancellor Paterson Library's resources. Thunder Bay Fire Rescue has to approve this plan; however, Lakehead University is accountable for ensuring the accuracy and completeness of data given in this fire plan.

This fire plan contains the following data: contact details, building resources audit, building resources maintenance (as requested by the Ontario Fire Code), construction schedules and duties, emergency processes, fire control and extinction, fire avoidance measures and fire risks.

The fire safety system is activated by:

- Manual pull stations
- Smoke detectors
- Duct smoke detectors
- Heat detectors
- Standpipe Flow Switch

Activation of the fire alarm system

- The security office will receive a fire alarm signal and its announcer panel is verified. An autonomous off-site surveillance station shall be equally transferred to a fire alarm signal.
- The Fire Alarm Advertiser and control panel displays the area data.

- Smoke-detectors are fitted with air handling units.

The entire building, situated in the duct, is present with fire dampers. Thermal dampers work and are not linked to the fire alarm system.

Importance of Fire Drills

Fire drills are frequently performed to guarantee that the fire evacuation processes are known to all construction occupants. In revising and refinement of fire emergency processes, fire drills help security services and human resources personnel.

The safest library has planned fire exercises annually, and records of fire exercises must be kept for one year. Every effort is produced in planning fire exercises so that the trials are inconsistent. During planned examination periods, drills will not happen.

All construction occupants must instantly evacuate during a fire exercise Building occupants must report to a Fire Warden any observations made during their evacuation. Any issues during the evacuation drill should be reported by Fire Wardens to Health & Safety by telephone.

REVIEW QUESTIONS

1. Explain preventive measures and its methods involved in environmental factors.
2. Define preventive measures of biological and chemical factors.
3. List out various methods involved in disaster preparedness/ response.
4. Explain care and handling?
5. Steps involved in care and handling of library resources.

4

Non-book Materials and their Preservation

LEARNING OBJECTIVES

After reading this Unit, you will be able to:

- To understand the nature and characters of the materials of which these are composed;
- Describe the technology involved in recording information on them; and
- Discuss the procedures relating to their care, handling and storage from the point of view of their proper preservation and use.

4.1. VARIETY OF NON-BOOK MATERIALS

Introduction

We are currently in a time where 'data' assumes a job substantially more indispensable than even previously. In the development of our Society the impact of 'data' is developing each day, both vertical and extent. The developing data advances today challenge our libraries to react to quick technological innovations. The libraries can never again stay unaffected and keep on limiting their extent of exercises basing on just the customary paper based media (which have been talked about. in detail in the preceding Unit).

Therefore, the present libraries are having consistently developing assortment of materials, other than paper. These falls under a by and large acknowledged conventional term: non-book materials. In the previous days, be that as it may, by non-book we implied those media, which were all paper-based, yet issued in configurations other than of an ordinary books, for example, periodicals, reports, flyers, papers, news cut-outs, maps, chart books, etc.

That differentiation among book and non-book is no longer in vogue on account of the attack of an umpteen number of items printed or recorded somehow or another or other on materials other than paper, and these non-paper items in the present setting are named 'non-book'.

What Are Non Book Marerials?

Non-book products are other than books in the library. They are materials not completely dependent on printed words for data and information transmission. In addition, materials are also needed for data, sound and information supply, such as projectors, computers, etc.

Categories of Non Book Materials

1. Cartographic materials : These are two Or three dimensional objects which are used representing the whole or partof the earth surface or any celestial body.

Examples are: Maps Globe Atlas House plans

2. Microforms : These are small-scale photographic papers. They are not visible with naked eyes, so devices called micro readers must be given. Normally they bring in their printed form what already exists. Microfilm,

Microfile, Microcard are examples.

3. Serials : These papers contain numerical or chronological designations in any media which are published in consecutive sections and which should be verified indeterminately. They are further split into journals and non-periodicals according to the specified frequency.

Examples include: Journals, magazines, newsletters, the congress, annual reports and monographs.

4. Sound Recordings : Information material is especially helpful for hearing users or users with partial hearing impairment. The sounds recorded on recordings or compact disks are the audio recording. You can be in a single track where one record is created or you can have a amount of tracks that match the amount of records. Special equipment, such as audio players, radio and tape recorders is needed for audio recording. Examples are: Mp3 (compact disc) tape cassette Cd

Diffeerence between Books and Non Book Materials

Any book that has a set of 49 pages or more, which are linked with a unique title is described as any printed document. It is a collection of paper sheets bound on one edge. On the other side, non-book materials are materials which do not depend entirely on printed words. In order to use them, they need extra infrastructure (computers).

Why Non Book Materials are Special Materials

Because of the formats and data they contain, non-book materials are unique materials in the library. Books made them the most popular library material, accounting for over 70 percent of the complete library collection. Fortunately, many data resources now appear in digitalized formats in electronic formats, making them unique with the introduction of ICT. In contrast to comics that do not require a specific machine before they are used, they involve unique equipment and instruments for use.

People believe that the format and mode of presentation they have come up with and are used for their specialty. They differ from books by lacking some of the fundamental features of a book like amount of pages, authorship, format and usage–all of which have specialized them.

This presently utilized conventional term 'non-book' incorporates two general classes: print and non-print. The non-print media, as apart from print-media, are those on which printed words or visuals are not straightforwardly presented to, for example, magnetic tapes, computerized records and so forth, as against media like movies. Film-strips, photos, slide and so on which bear the immediate impressions of words or visuals. Non-book materials which are commonly accessible in our libraries today can be categorized as follows:

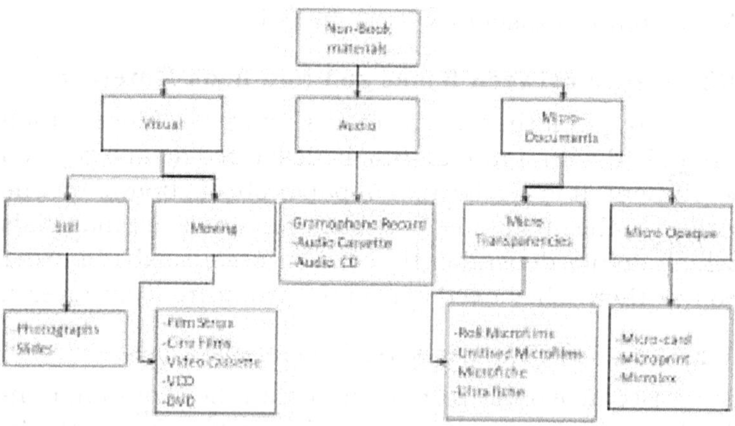

Fig. 1. Non-Book Materials in Libraries

4.2. PHYSICAL ENVIRONMENT FOR STORING OF NON-BOOK MATERIALS

Non-book materials comprise of periodicals, newspapers, flyers, maps, photos, pictures, posters, slides, film strips, movies, video tapes, audio tapes, microfilms and microfiches, PC plates, and so forth.

Today, as a data service, a library isn't efficient in the event that it doesn't make a portion of these materials accessible to its clients. It is additionally accepted that NGOs overall get a portion of the previously mentioned materials which is the reason they must be managed here as well.

4.2.1. Accessions book for non-book materials

With the exception of periodicals, pamphlets and clippings, all non-book materials ought to be gone into an access book. All together not to stir up books and reports with non-book materials, begin a different promotions book with discrete areas for various materials, for instance:

- photographs (Ph)
- slides (S)
- video tapes (V)
- motion pictures/films (F)
- sound recordings (C)
- microfiches and/or microfilms (M)
- posters (Po).

In each part the accession number begins with 1 and will be prefixed by the symbol (the capital letter appeared above in sections) for the particular sort of material. The 21st tape or sound tape in your library will hence get the number C-21.

For the above recorded non-book materials the accession number fills both area and allocation needs.

4.2.2. Storage of non-book materials

The storage of non-book materials varies incredibly from that of books. They regularly require extraordinary treatment and storage offices, for example, vertical documents, hanging/suspending records, extraordinarily planned cabinets, shelves and cases. Safe storage of some non-book materials (for example films, video tapes, movies, plates) requires an exceptional climate. Mugginess, dryness and temperature ought to be with the end goal that they don't harm the materials. In the accompanying sections it is conceivable to give just broad rules and indications. For guidance on how best to store and secure your materials you ought to ask locally.

The selection strategies for all kinds of libraries—government libraries, educational libraries, technical college libraries and school libraries (government or private)-should provide guidelines for experts to make informed decisions. The resource selection procedure should be guided by criteria. Criteria for choosing products in all subject fields and formats should be to mix general, particular, and technical. In relation to criteria like age and customer level, librarians must also consider developing a collection that represents a range of thoughts and writers and represents the population of the library.

Guidance on Selection Criteria : Special criteria for guiding experts in buying products should be included in the selection policy. Criteria should apply to the goals of the library: excellence (artistic, literary, visual), user-level suitability, the authoritative and diverse views on contentious problems, accessibility and the capacity to encourage further intellectual and social development. The authenticity, government demand, overall interest, content, and usage conditions are something for librarians to consider. Librarians should consider age, social and emotional growth, level of intellectual concern and reading for libraries serving minors. Technical criteria (such as audio clarity, film quality and graphics quality in games) should also be included in the policy.

Public Library Selection Criteria : Taking a variety of criteria into consideration, public libraries can generate a community collection that uses their resources to best advantage. There are overall selection criteria, but the comparative significance of those criteria for their society will need to be determined by each organisation. These considerations serve as guidelines when making choices on ways to best invest resources to maximize the effect of the library collection in general, specific and/or unique to particular collections. These considerations are

There is a wide variety of public libraries and the wide population. Selection criteria should take into consideration the diverse concerns and needs of the library's owners, with a client base that may include children from the elderly. The selection criteria for the products should rely on the objectives and task of the library / system. Public libraries generally offer collections that contain a range of material sizes, including print, audio-visual and electronic materials. The library personnel select and develop materials for adults, kids and adolescents to include materials that reflect a variety of human experiences, not only the region of their region but also a broader worldwide outlook, reflecting ethnic, religious, racist, and socio-economic diversity. A wide variety of opinions on present problems will be provided by the Library Collections.

The collections comprise famous works, classical works, and other materials of particular concern that have withstood the test of time. Works based exclusively on topics or on political, religious or ideological basis are not excluded or incorporated into the collection. Library employees in construction collections are driven not by censorship, but by the principle of choice. In addition, it should not be interpreted as a support of one specific point of view when selecting a specified object for the library collection.

Differences Between Notation and Index

Notation is a word used in the grading timetable. Notation is a number of symbols used to represent a topic and is an extremely significant characteristic of a library classification. As per W. As per W. Howard Phillips, "Book notations are a sequence of symbols that represent the name of a class, a division or subdivision of a class, and are forms of a useful reference to the structure of the classification. It comprises of a mixture of 3 to 4 digits of letters that refers to the classification system of the library. Therefore, the notation is also called the' classification mark.' In the classification scheme all ratings are described. For a subject search the notation can be used in the library catalog, as books on the same topic are devoted to the same notation. For the practical application of the classification of books, a note is thus essential; without a note the classification could never be used for books. Since classification is the "foundation of the libraries," "notation is the basis for practical classification of books."

Today, the proliferation of non print (NPM) products, for example, audio visual materials, electronic materials, etc. There is something new and revolutionary in non-print format every day, and both the teacher and the librarian cannot just think in terms of books. In explaining the distinct media collections, the literature contains a variety of terms such as non-prints, non-book materials, audio visual materials, etc. However, there are restrictions to each term. This word has been sought by many experts on numerous occasions. According to Feather and Sturges, "Audio visual components is a general word to describe data contents that contain pictures and sound rather than or are sometimes used in relation to textual matter in storage and transmission media or formats. This involves audio CD, records and tapes. The formats that combine two or more of the formats include photography, slides, films, and videos. Many of these formats now have been removed. "(Feather and Sturges 2003). However, only audiocassettes, videocassettes, movie images, slides, Microforms and CD ROMs are included in the non-print resources for this article.

Pattern of Access of Non-print Materials : The accessibility of non-print materials is a further significant problem for the librarian. In order to guarantee appropriate safety, avoid continuous processing and consequent harm, some libraries prefer closed access. Others prefer open access because self-publishing attracts the attention of individuals who may not be conscious of their presence (Lawal 2002). The current trend is to open access however, which makes partial integration easier and discourages the misconception that non-print resources are unique materials requiring unique therapy.

4.2.3. Cataloguing and filing of catalogue cards of non-book materials

By and large, most non-book materials are listed by similar guidelines related to books. For subtleties see the accompanying parts.

Yet, there are variances in documenting the index cards. The cards of those materials to which you appointed a class number should, obviously, be recorded in the ordered list. The call number for non-book materials contrasts from the one for books, and in this way it is prudent to put the list cards for non-book materials at the end part of the arrangement. In the event that you have an extensive number of inventoried non-book materials in your library it is better to hold one cabinet of your catalogue bureau for the cards of non-book materials and to record the index cards as indicated by the sort of materials in numerical request of accession numbers, e.g. Cassette/C-1 to Cassette/C-14 or Photo/Ph-1 to Photo/Ph-78. Do not forget to insert guide cards and to label the drawer appropriately.

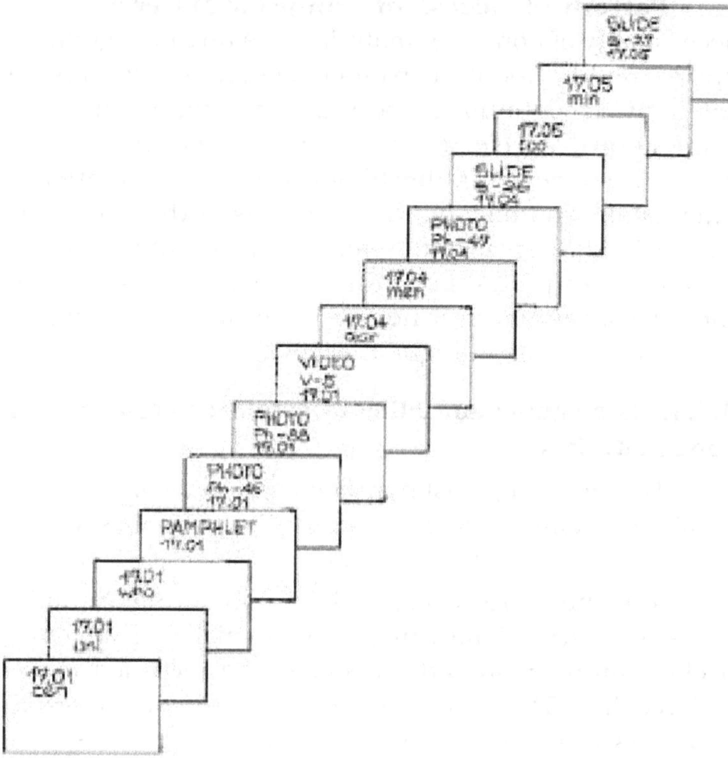

Fig. 2

In the event that there are writer and title cards for non-book materials they ought to be recorded together with the index cards for books in the particular card inventories.

As to the title inventory please recall that there is no sense in setting up a catalogue card for a title which you created as-will be the situation with photos, slides, handout documents, and so on.

4.2.4. Periodicals

The term periodical incorporates journals, magazines, and pamphlets (with the exception of day by day ones, for example newspapers) which are distributed successively and at standard timings. Periodicals are a significant wellspring of data for all documentation focuses as they are more present and updated than books. In the field of provincial improvement and proper innovation, there are numerous periodicals which might be acquired for nothing out of pocket. In any case, be mindful so as not to gather too much. Prior to requesting any new periodical, give it however and examine the issue with your associates. Consider that time and space is expected to utilize these periodicals.

For every periodical a record card (likewise called "checking card") is utilized to enter each issue as it is gotten. The record card ought to be 15 cm X 21 cm. By utilizing a genuinely huge size it tends to be utilized for some volumes or years. Any nearby printer can print such cards yet you can likewise make them yourself on the off chance that you needn't bother with more than around 20 duplicates, (see Fig). The back of the card should be left blank for notes, e.g.

- How long will the periodical be kept? (indefinitely, 5/4/3/2/1 years, current issue only)
- If kept indefinitely complete volume to be bound? yes/no
- Display on the display shelf? yes/no
- To whom will it be circulated regularly? (circulation list)

The record cards are kept in a separate card tray and filed in alphabetical order by title.

Usually, periodicals are not classified and categorised since the record card is already there. Essential articles should be replicated and filed in the separate pamphlets file.

If you do not need to reproduce the article you can also state the user openly to the article by arranging a reference card for the file (Fig.4.3). The consumer will thus recognise that he will catch the article in the magazine "The Courier" and not on the shelves.

15.06
tro

TROPICAL OILSEEDS

see: The Courier. No. 86, July-Aug.
1964, page 52-93.

Fig. 3. Cataloguing periodicals

In special cases, a special sum of a journal which pleasures an only subject of reputation to your library can be given as a monograph, i.e. catalogued and categorised, and put on the shelves. In such an occasion, it is logical to replicate the first page, note down the call figure and case it in the corresponding magazine package to elude a search for that particular number.

4.2.4.1. Storage of periodicals

Periodicals are best put away in an exceptionally structured box called a 'magazine box' or a 'pamphlet record'. Bulletins which come without a packing and comprise of a couple of pages just are best put away in free leaf folios as they get tampered instantly whenever put into boxes. The periodicals are labelled with ownership, put into boxes or records and allocated in sequential design by title in a unique segment of the racks. Each container/document ought to be obviously set apart with the title and the volume(s) it contains.

See the following pages for a sample for record cards (size: 15 × 21 cm).

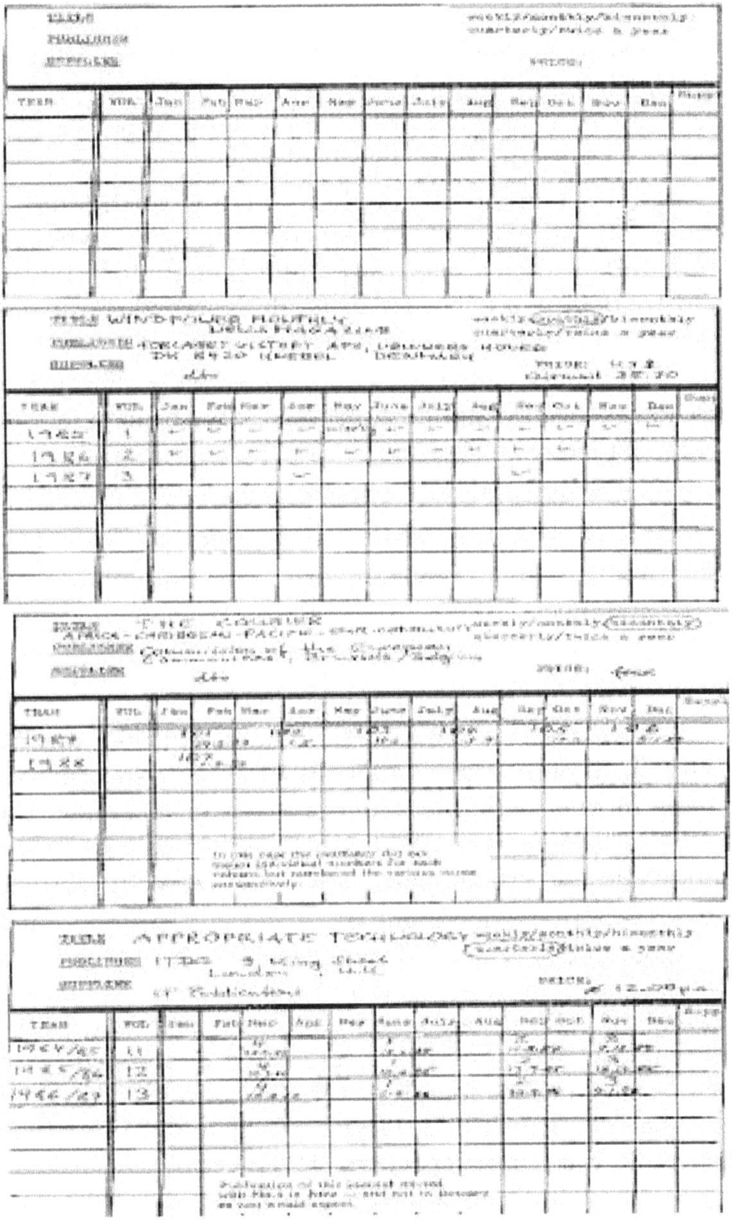

Fig. 4. Record card for periodicals

4.2.5. Pamphlets

The meaning of a pamphlet is most importantly dependent on its structure, for example that it is a printed work not for all time bound. Pamphlets regularly give more recent exceptional data than books.

A few pamphlets may have lasting worth (and an extensive number of pages) regardless of whether unbound. In such a case, the pamphlet ought to be bound and treated as a book, for example recorded, arranged, given a call number and put on the racks.

All others which are either excessively slim (just a few pages) or too unimportant to possibly be kept forever will most likely comprise of:

- Important articles from journals,
- Short project reports or other project documents,
- leaflets about specific products and plants for instance,
- Leaflets about organizations,
- Or any other unbound material.

What's more, some of the time it very well may be valuable to photocopy significant letters and incorporate them in the pamphlets document, for example the responses to enquiries your association has sent to the inquiry and-answer administration of associations abroad.

Pamphlets don't get an accession number and normally they are not indexed. Albeit no inventory cards will be set up for them, you in any case need to choose a branch of topic so as to document them effectively in the pamphlets records. The archives are stepped with possession and set apart with the class number. The class number comes after "PAMPHLET". The pamphlets are then placed in the pamphlet record. The pamphlet record can have the type of a loose-leaf binder or of a magazine box. It relies upon the measure of pamphlets you are probably going to get whether you get ready pamphlet documents for the particular full scale class number just or whether you allot them explicit class numbers, as well.

When you begin setting up your library it may be adequate to introduce one document just for all pamphlets inside a given full scale collection. Be that as it may, every pamphlet is by and by altogether grouped, for example whenever required down to the third level-however not catalogued!

On the off chance that you later discover that it will be increasingly fitting to likewise have pamphlet documents for some important bunches regardless you can still partition the record. Such as: One pamphlet record has been set up for the whole gathering 05.00 "governmental issues, Public Administration, Law and Legislation". After some time you find that it is smarter to have a different document for "Human Rights". You just take out those pamphlets managing human rights from the general legislative issues document and place them into the new record on human rights. No progressions are required on the index cards (if the pamphlets have been inventoried) since the archives have just been ordered with "05.04 - Human Rights".

For every pamphlet record a rundown of subject matters ought to be arranged and put on to the back of the title page. It is valuable to number the pamphlets inside each document.

For each pamphlet file one catalogue card only will be prepared and filed in the classified card catalogue, for example:

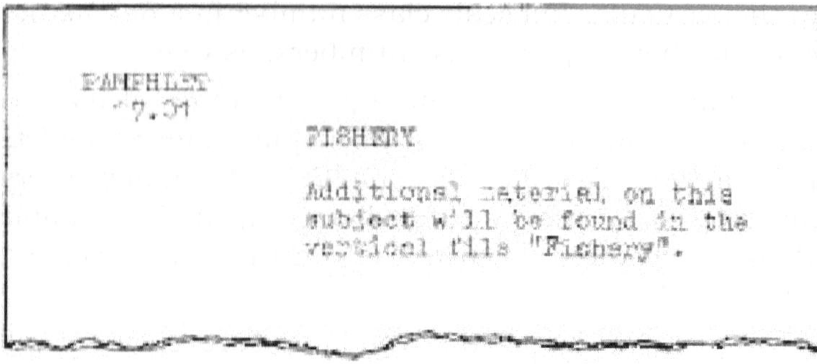
PAMPHLET
7.01
FISHERY
Additional material on this subject will be found in the vertical file "Fishery".

Fig. 5. Cataloguing pamphlets

A portion of the pamphlets which are not to be bound but rather which are placed in the pamphlets record should all things considered be classified on the off chance that they are vital to your library. They ought to be indexed and categorized as depicted in Chapters 3 and 5. Be that as it may, the call number is again gone before by "PAMPHLET" so as to allude the client to its area, for example the pamphlet document.

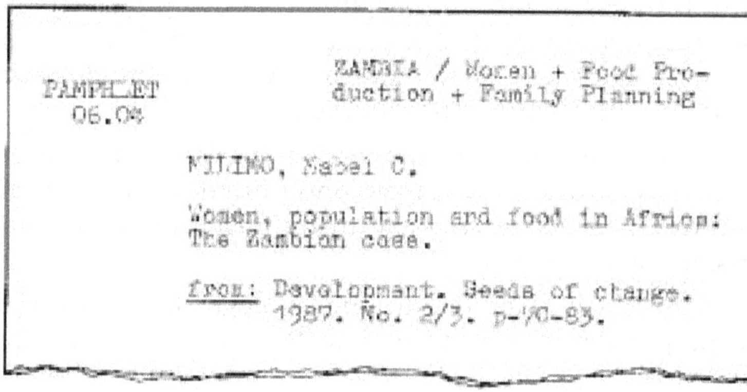
PAMPHLET
06.04
ZAMBIA / Women + Food Production + Family Planning
MILIMO, Mabel C.
Women, population and food in Africa: The Zambian case.
from: Development. Seeds of change. 1987. No. 2/3. p-70-83.

Fig. 6. Cataloguing pamphlet

The catalogue cards books.

Another approach to store pamphlets is by utilizing hanging records (likewise called suspending documents) which are named with the reacting class number. The upside of hanging records is that they spare space and that storage and documenting are somewhat quicker since the reports don't need to be punched.

The inconvenience is that they are more costly than loose-leaf folios and that you additionally need a hanging file cupboard. Another difficulty is that the pamphlets are subsequently isolated from the books which mean the client needs to scan in two unique areas for applicable data.

Since a portion of the pamphlets are of brief worth just to your library you should weed the documents at ordinary breaks (when a year ought to be adequate) and take out each one of those which are never again required.

4.2.6. Newspaper Clippings

Clippings/cuttings from papers are a significant wellspring of data for any documentation centre. They are especially significant for units gaining practical experience in gathering data about their very own nation since data on current advancements of a nation for the most part is first distributed in papers.

The papers to which your association buys in are to be checked routinely for articles of conceivable importance to your association's work. As it very well may be assumed that the majority of the staff individuals will likewise peruse the papers, you ought to request that they imprint articles to be removed and kept. At usual intervals (commonly once every week) you should remove the checked articles and include the source (the paper's name) and the date. Make sure to remove the total article-frequently articles are preceded on another page and one can without much of a stretch neglect to cut that part as well. The clippings are then stuck on a sheet of paper (once more: remember to include the source and the date) and arranged by their primary subject. The class number or the subject, for example "Transport", "Environment", "Solar based Energy", "Contamination Control", "General Election", or "Political Party" are then composed at the highest point of the sheet.

Clippings might be either put away in an explicitly stamped segment of the pamphlets document or put away independently in hanging records. When a year the records ought to be checked and all clippings never again required ought to be gotten rid of.

In the event that you keep up a genuinely huge clipping service, it is valuable to have stamps with the name of the paper. It makes your work simpler, quicker and tidier.

4.2.7. Maps

Maps are another significant wellspring of data. They come in a wide range of structures: little or enormous level maps, divider maps, and collapsed maps, (for example, travel or guides). In the event that conceivable you should crease the level maps so that they fit into boxes the size of the magazine boxes.

The territory secured is the most significant and essential methodology; thusly it is suggested that maps be entered under the region secured.

On the off chance that a guide has both topographical and subject perspectives, the geological viewpoint is viewed as the vital one. The principle heading will in this manner be the territory secured. The subject viewpoint is viewed as auxiliary and will in this way be secured by an optional class number.

Example: A geologic map of Nepal will be placed by a Nepalese library with 01.03.01/NEP, the secondary class number will be 10.07 (= Geology).

The Rural Development Classification Model provides one class "01.03" for maps. If you have maps of your country and other parts of the world as well, you can subdivide the class for maps as follows:

01.03 Maps, Atlases (world and/or continents)

01.03.01 Maps, Atlases of . . . (here follows the name of your country)

01.03.02 Maps, Atlases of other countries

In the case of maps, the call number is controlled of the class number and the first three letters of the area enclosed and entered in capital letters to differentiate it from the call number for volumes.

01.03 (= class number)

NEP (= first three letters of the area covered)

In cataloguing the following information should be given:

1. Call number
2. Area covered (in capital letters)
3. Title of the map
4. Author/designer/cartographer (if mentioned)
5. Publisher or issuing body
6. Date
7. Scale
8. Size (in cm or inches)

For examples of how to catalogue maps see Figs. 4.6 + 4.7.

01.03
MAN

MANILA

City map of Manila and suburbs. Covers:
City of Manila, Makati, Pasay City,
parts of Caloocan City, Quezon City,
Mandaluyong. (incl. street index).
Cartogr. Design: H. Engeler.
1:12,500. On the back: Metro Manila,
scale 1:250,000.
Manila: National Bookstore 1982.
72.5 x 102 cm

Fig. 7. Cataloguing maps

4.2.8. Photographs

Photos of the assignment area, the objective gathering and the work in advancement are significant guides for the documentation of undertaking exercises. So as to furnish the clients with the most ideal data these photographs ought to likewise be incorporated into the library's gathering which implies that they are to be inventoried.

The arrangements of photos (in uncommon cases single photos) will be entered in the accessions book for non-book materials in the structure appeared in Fig. 4.8. The passage ought to contain a note whether the negatives are likewise accessible. A similar number ought to consistently be appointed to the arrangement of photos and the negatives.

So as to effectively recognize the index cards for photos from the ones for books and records the code "Photo" is added to the call number

Photo

Ph-35

The call number for photographs is thus composed of the word "Photo" and the accession number only.

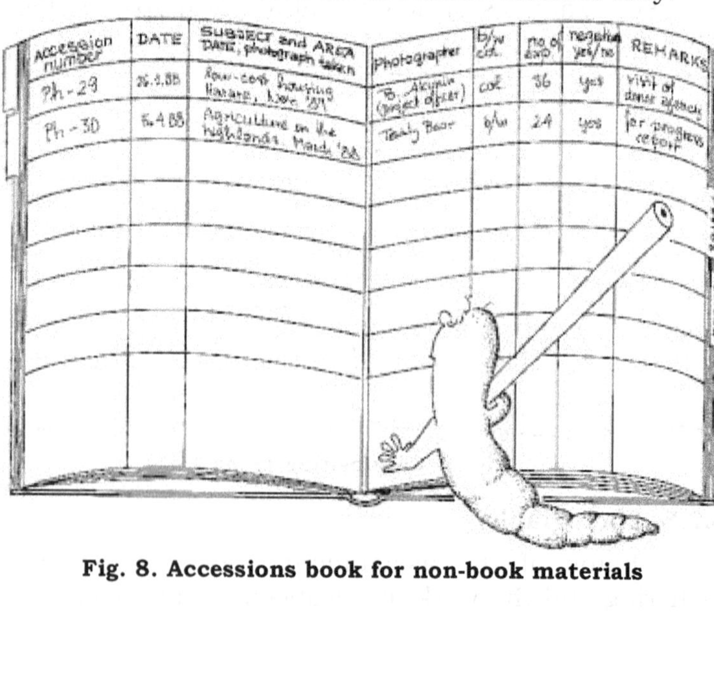

Fig. 8. Accessions book for non-book materials

With photographs, the matter area concealed is possibly more vital to the user than the topographical area, and therefore the focal headline will be the topic. As pictures do not arise with a stable title you invent one, humbly select the main subject as the label or practice the name of the assignment as the heading. The physical depiction of prints embraces the following components:

1. Title/subject
2. Photographer (if known)
3. Short description (area and subjects covered)
4. Date
5. Number in a set
6. Size
7. Black and white or colour (b/w or colt)
8. Accession number

For an example of how to catalogue photographs see Fig. 4.9.

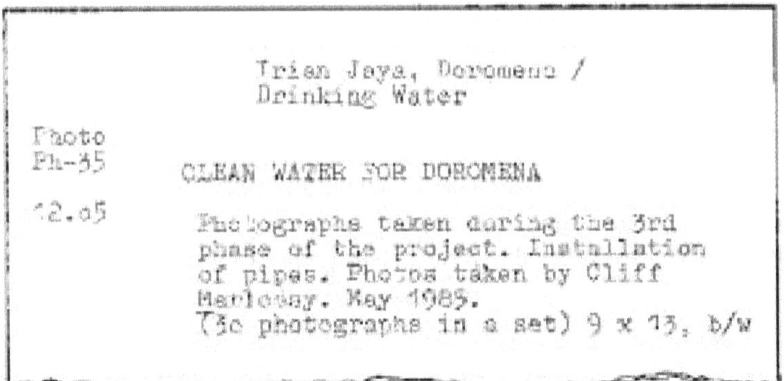
Trian Jaya, Doromena /
Drinking Water

Photo
Ph-35
12.05

CLEAN WATER FOR DOROMENA

Photographs taken during the 3rd
phase of the project. Installation
of pipes. Photos taken by Cliff
Marlowey. May 1985.
(30 photographs in a set) 9 x 13, b/w

Fig. 9. Cataloguing photographs

4.2.8.1. Storage

Before loading the pictures the location, topic and date should be noticeable on the back of respective photograph (if possible by the photographer himself/herself!). It is suitable to stand them on mounting panel or simple white paper; the place, subject and date had better be printed on the mounting panel.

In minor collections, i.e. if it is supplementary or less the exception to have prints and photographic documentation is generally done with slides, prints are best trooped in the proper pamphlets file (the file that corresponds with the class number).

However in the event that several photographs are saved, a distinct photograph case may be formed. One can either put them in hanging files or in wrappings that will be retained in steel filing cabinet or stock them in minor albums which are delivered free of cost in some nations by photo shops. In all cases the loading unit (file/ envelope/album) should be discernable with the call number, the topic and the date and organised by accession number.

Negatives, i.e. the roll of developed film, cannot be put away in the same place as the photos. The negatives should be deposited in a cool and dim apartment, if at all possible in a steel filing cabinet, and allocated in arithmetic order conferring to accession number.

4.2.9. Slides

Slides are habitually preserved in slide trays or crystal clear slide cases and deposited separately from books in cupboards. They are generally come in under the label which at times you might have to design. Slides are also entered in the accessions book, the accession number is preceded by an "S". For sorting and loading see also Chapter 4.2.8 "Photographs".

Tanzania / Sisal

Slide
S-41 SISAL PRODUCTION (Slides)

Sisal production in the Tanga region /
15.13 Tanzania. Prepared by TEC.
50 slides, col., 5 x 5 cm

Fig. 10. Cataloguing slides (fictitious examples)

Slide
S- 22 PROJECT RECONSTRUCTION SAIGHANCHI
AFGHANISTAN (Slides)

2?.07 Earthquake resisting building system.
Produced by Australian Council of
Churches et al. (1980 ?)
80 slides, col., 5 x 5 cm
1 cassette, 60 min.

Fig. 11. Cataloguing a sound and slide show

Audio and slide presentations which generally consist of a regular order of slides and an accompanying audio cassette or tape must be entered below slides, as it can be assumed that the slides are more imperative than the cassette/tape.

4.2.10. Sound Recordings

As it can be anticipated that in a small library the most of recordings, if there are any at all, comprise of audial cassettes (conventional songs, lectures, interviews, etc.), we will only work with them and not with phonodiscs even though there are only minor modifications in categorisation.

Yet again, entirely cassettes must be entered in the distinct section for tapes in the accessions book. They are finest established by accession number and preserved in a show tray or some fitting box which then is stockpiled in four drawer cupboards or any other filing cabinet.

In cataloguing cassettes the following information should be given:

1. Title
2. Author, i.e. composer and/or singer, lecturer
3. Publisher
4. Date (if available)
5. Stereo or mono
6. Playing time in minutes

There are no secure procedures for sound tapes as to which portion is to be regarded as the foremost header. It can be the musician, the interpreter (singer, vocalist, soloist, or orchestra) or the title. You ought to select yourself how to enter a cassette, reliant on where the consumers will believe to catch it.

For examples of how are catalogue cassettes see Fig. 4.12 + 4.13.

```
Cassette
 C- 56      MAMBESAK

 06.12      Seri lagu-lagu rakyat "Iriani".
            Vol. 1 (Irianese folksongs)
            Jayapura: Lembaga Antropologi/UNCEN
            1979.  60 min.
```

Fig. 12. Cataloguing cassettes (music)

```
Cassette
 C - 75     MANANZAN, Mary John Sr

            Women and technology. An outline.
06.04       Recording of a lecture given in
            July 1986 during the Intern. Consul-
            tation "Toward A Common Sharing Of
            Technology" in Manila / Philippines.
            Manila: SEARICE 1986.  60 min.
```

Fig. 13. Cataloguing cassettes (lecture)

4.2.11. Video Tapes and Motion Pictures (Films)

Film tapes and motion pictures/films come into their label, tailed by the caption and the description "Video" or "Motion Picture". On the index card the following material will be given:

1. Title and subtitle
2. Sponsor
3. Producer
4. Director
5. Date
6. Running time in minutes (min.)
7. Number of reels or cassettes
8. Indication of sound (sd) or silent (si)
9. Indication of colour (col.) or black and white (b/w)
10. Width in mm
11. Technical system or trade name (for videos only)

For an example of how to catalogue a video tape see Fig. 4.14. For an example of how to catalogue a motion picture see Fig. 4.15.

Video
V - 5

SHEA BUTTER PROCESSING IN MALI (Video)

15.06

Sponsor: German Appropriate Technology Exchange (GATE), Eschborn. Director: Peter Bolelmann.
1986. 1 cassette, 34 min., sd, col., VHS

Fig. 14. Cataloguing a video tape

```
Film
F-6       THE SWEET STINGER. (Motion picture)

16.10     On the beekeeping project Boabeng-Fiema,
          Ghana.) Sponsor: German Appropriate
          Technology Exchange (GATE). Producer:
          N.A.F.T.I. (Ghana Film Institute).
          Director: Mr. Frimpong - Boakye.
          1987. 1 reel, 32 min, sd, col., 16 mm
```

Fig. 15. Cataloguing a motion picture

The accession number of a audio-visual tape is headed by a "V" and the call number by "VIDEO", for example:

VIDEO

V-6

The accession number of a motion picture/film is preceded by an "F" and the call number by "FILM", for example:

FILM

F-2

Videocassette tapes and motion pictures are organised by accession number. They must be deposited in multi-drawer cupboards. Moisture should not be too great as then the films will be impaired by fungus and mould. Alternatively, too much dryness makes films to curl and turn brittle.

4.2.12. Posters and Charts

For scholastic resolves some establishments keep pictures and charts (flipcharts). When sorting these constituents the succeeding fundamentals must be included:

1. Author/editor
2. Title/subject (incl. short description)

3. Place of publication
4. Publisher
5. Date of publication
6. Size
7. Black and white or colour

For a made-up sample of how to index posters see Fig. 4.16.

The calmest and economical tactic to store posters and charts is to reel them up and to preserve the rolls in packages. Nonetheless there are also flat file cupboards specifically planned for large materials.

```
Poster
Po - 4      WORLD HEALTH ORGANIZATION (WHO)

            Common medicinal plants in Sri Lanka.
13.07.02    Set of posters.
            Colombo: WHO 1986. 5 sheets, 91 x 120 cm
            col.
```

Fig. 16. Cataloguing posters

4.2.13. Microfiche/Computer Disks

As small libraries are further expected to retain microfiches than microfilms, if at all, we will deal only with microfiches. Microfiches are recorded agreeing to the rules for the material of which they are a replica, i.e. books, periodicals or leaflets. But the description "Microfiche" is entered into the name and in the collection area indication must be made of the number of cards/microfiches. The accession number is preceded by an "M". If your library has the key file, allusion should be finished on the index card for the manuscript that a microfiche copy is also presented; and on the directory card for the microfiche that the original file is open in the library.

It is prudent to accumulate microfiches in cases specifically planned for this resolution. The microfiche provider will be capable to tell you where to obtain these storage cartons.

Computer disks and software drivers must only be arranged if your library has a substantial collection of documents in this standard. But they nevertheless are stated here then they create a new form of storing material. It is self-evident that disks should be sensibly categorised and stockpiled. A variation of disk files/boxes is available on the markets which protect them from dust and agency mishaps. It is advisable to buy ones which can be sealed.

4.3. CARE AND HANDLING OF NON-BOOK MATERIALS

For maintenance and handling of audio-visual materials, several standards, such as, International (ISO), British (BSI), American (ANSI) and German (DIN) already exist. Several of the audio-visuals archives links have also formed draft procedures on management and preservation. There is, in fact, no dearth of recommendations, but most of these guidelines and Ethics deal with packing, fire protections, specifications for film and photographic bases, and exhibitions. These guidelines are, no doubt, advantageous, but those can only be taken as non-comprehensive, interim measures. The long-standing competence of some of these preparations is yet to be conclusively established, because the inherent durability of the materials has not yet been fully established. However, there are certain basic concerns, which are applicable to all non-book materials, as are for book-materials, and are well established principles from the preservation point of view. These are concerned with physical environment, security and rotation.

REVIEW QUESTIONS

1. The categories of non-book materials available in the libraries are:

   (a) Visual

   (b) Still photographs, slides, etc.

(c) Moving - Film-strips, cine films, video cassettes and disc.

(d) Audio

(e) Sound recording, gramophone record, compact disc (CD),

(f) Digital audio technology (DAT), Audio tape, audio cassette.

(g) Microforms

2. The different types of film media are:

   (a) film strip

   (b) slides

   (c) cinefilms

   (d) microforms

3. Do's:

   (a) Microforms should be stored in air conditioned room having temperature of 20-22 degree Celsius and relative humidity of 45-50 per cent.

   (b) Keep microforms in closed drawer type cabinets and shelve them upright in a vertical position.

   Don'ts:

   (a) Do not store nitrate based films and acetate/polyester films together.

   (b) Do not touch information content area of microforms. This may damage the information.

Magnetic media are non-archival storage devices having stability of recorded information between 10-20 years. The magnetic media are vulnerable to accidental erasure by a sufficiently coercive opposite magnetic force. Also, inter-layer transfer, improper handling, media wear and environmental conditions can considerably affect the stability of information in magnetic media.

5

Current Trends in Preserving the Library Materials

LEARNING OBJECTIVES

After reading this Unit, you will be able to:

- Describe the digital preservation and its need.
- Explain the role of international/national organizations.
- To understand the nature and characters of the materials of which these are composed;
- Explain the Indian initiatives towards digital preservation

5.1. DIGITAL PRESERVATION AND ITS NEED

Introduction

"Digital conservation covers a wide variety of operations, to ensure that machine readable computer files are ready for use and safeguards against media failure, physical loss and obsolescence," Cornell University Library says.

According to Russell (1998), the Digital Preservation process is a digital approach that enables digital data to be perceived to ensure that the information contained therein is usable, durable and has intellectual integrity.

5.1.1. Concept of Digital Preservation

Digital preservation is usually a result of the use of one or more digital preservation strategies in the long term for storage, maintenance and accessibility of a digital material. These approaches include preserving technology, emulating technology, or migrating dates.

5.1.2. Objectives of Digital Preservation

Digital preservation is mainly based on the following objectives:

- Providing continued access to digital material for digital materials as well as for digital materials. The digital preservation is primary to achieve the following objectives.
- Ensure that the digital material preserved is authentic.
- Preserve physical media to ensure environmental control to prevent damage / deterioration.
- Changes to new and fresher digital data where required.
- Coordinating all the global conservation initiatives, with a view to increasing synergies, avoiding redundancies and reducing costs. This offers an efficient cooperation infrastructure through the connection of various networks, organizations and people involved.
- Concentrate the stakeholders on matters that need to be addressed urgently. It is the fundamental hypothesis that action must be taken at the beginning and not in secondary phases.

5.1.3. Requirements of Digital Preservation

Digital preservation combines policies, strategies and measures to guarantee that digital objects are genuine, available and maintained for long-term customers and systems irrespective of component difficulties and management errors, natural disasters or assaults.

However, the requirements for all digital preservation are not definable as, for instance, the type, the size and the quantity of the data depend on digital preservation. It also relies on every organization's objectives in terms of information reuse. There are however several generic and common conditions, depending on the data stored today, which somebody would in future requiring.

1. Digital conservation needs that any digital object preserved is unknown but may be copied (or maintained) for decades or even centuries.. It can be described as a necessity for reliability. A digital conservation scheme must therefore be intended to store information forever without loss of information.

2. If the accessed data is trustworthy enough, a potential customer should be able to decide. This typically involves ensuring the authenticity of digital objects (which is already a prevalent necessity for concrete objects). The provenance of digital objects, in particular the creator or entity responsible for them, should also be needed. In addition, it is important to ensure the integrity of digital objects, to ensure that their information content has not been modified.

3. Digital preservation calls on potential customers to receive the preserved data designed by their creators to deal with obsolescence threats. This requirement includes a number of difficulties because a digital object that needs to be explored need certain software and, in some case, evens certain hardware technological background.

4. Digital preservation dynamic collection and environments involve technological scalability to address technological developments, for example through incremental updates, to add fresh elements.
   - A set information size is available as a static collection, such as a digitized historical archive, where no fresh objects are added.
   - While additional parts will not be essential to boost storage ability, parts may have to be replaced by more modern technology (to reduce maintenance expenses or merely because the original technique has been broken down).

Fortunately, in digital preservation some typical storage systems requirements are not essential. For example, information updates are rare, because objects are normally expected to stay unchanged within digital conservation schemes. Almost all writing access is either to ingest fresh items or to rewrite newly migrated current objects.

5.1.4. Digitization Equipments

- Wide format scanner which can scan document width up to 42 inches
- Digital Cameras
- Scanners (8.5"x14") & Scanners (8.5 x 11.5)
- Book scanners with V shaped cradle
- Dark rooms with lighting equipment
- *Servers*: IBM server with an installed storage 0f 20TB, Scalable up to 48TB
- *Backup equipment*: LTOP Tap drives, hard drivers, DVD writers.
- *Computers*: Desktop and Laptops. These are required based on the available documents which are going to be digitized.

5.1.4.1. Methods of Digital Preservation

Digital preservation works to ensure that documents generated electronically by today's computer systems and apps are kept accessible, usable, and genuine in future use, so that digital preservation is more than a bit stream of documents to interpret record survival, otherwise the bit stream is nothing more than meaningless series of 0's and 1's without interpretation.

5.1.4.1.1. Preservation of Digital Materials

The digital media certainly have an enormous ability to capture data that enables consumers to access data without any appearance, but in contrast to print media it is very vulnerable. It is more complex to archive digital data than to archive printed data.

Digital preservation implies measures to guarantee the electronic document's longevity in accordance with the following.

- Data (for text, picture, video, or audio stored in a range of formats, standards)
- Data index
- Storage medium
- Other data link
- Metadata software (for hardware and operating system).

Hence, in the preservation of digital heritage material the following measures taken into account.

- Digital material integrity
- Physical presence
- Preservation size
- Functionality of digital components
- Material authenticity &
- Origin

5.1.4.1.2. Standards for Digital Preservation

Standardization is the secret to quality, measured uniformity, standards and terminology that directly influence mass production that contributes to the saving of time, space, effort, workforce, money, and facilitates and acts as an information transfer instrument needed to preserve digital data.

5.1.4.1.3. Standards for Architecture

Digital collection management cannot be the responsibility of just one central organization in a distributed digital environment. Concepts, definitions and procedure should be agreed in such a setting. For this purpose, the record management architecture contains several norms.

A. ISO/DIS 15489 : Such a draft international standard on registry management allows organization to standardize primarily for the design and execution of the registry scheme.

B. AS 4390 : Australia was the first nation in the globe to establish a record management standard in December 1995, i.e. AS 4390–1996 AS 4390. Following the approval and publication of the standard, work on the creation of an International Standard started on the global record management community.

C. DOD 5015.2.STD : The United States Defense Department is being created. Implementation of DOD 5015.2.STD and procedural guidelines for managing documents.

D. OAIS (Open Archival Information System) : It is established by the NASA Space Data System Advisory Committee (CC SCS). Both information flow and the archival requirements were described in the OAIS reference model and are being examined as ISO / DIS. Different kinds of digital library and archives implement this architecture.

5.1.4.1.4. Standards for Preservation content

Conservation content standards should depend on the aging phase of the semantic and physical recovery of the preserved document. A standard can provide such longevity only if it does not alter the standard itself and offers a backwards compatibility. XML and PDF are most often presented as two competitors in order to preserve a long-term document.

A. PDF (Portable Document Format) : PDF if Adobe is the owner of the standard document. The picture model of the post-script language is used for the accurate copying of the initial text and picture. Two format kinds are available in the PDF.

- Postscript font technique PDL (Page Description Language) for the page format description and
- Scanned picture PDI roster with no text contours font OCR

B. XML (eXtensible Mark-up Language) : XML is an SGml Standard SGML subset and is related to the HTML Hypertext Markup Language Web language (XML, 2001). With XML a specific type document known as a document type description (DTD) can save the structure of the document. You can use the document style sheet form specification. You can use the Cascading Style Booklet (CSS), XSL or XSL transformation style (XSLT). Finally, the document's contents can be saved with XML "tags" in ASCII format.

5.1.4.1.5. Standards for Preservation Access

The preservation of a bit stream from the document in a standard format is not enough to maintain a document for an indefinite period of time, therefore a file / formats which are stored at different physical places in the information system, and linked by cross reference, must be used to describe the digital, object or various parts in one object. These kinds of descriptions are known as metadata that includes contextual data for managing, collecting and interpreting additional electronic data.

A. Dublin Core : The Dublin core is designed particularly for discovery of cross-disciplinary networks. There are 15 components for description and discovery of assets (i.e. title, creator, subject, description, publisher, contributor, date, type, format, identifier, source, language, relation, cover and right).

B. MARC : MARC describes bibliographical and relational concept in machine-readable forms as representation and communication. Machine records have a guide to their information or a small "post sign".

C. Z39.50 : Z39.50 is the ANSI / NISO standard for the storage and collection of data under the Z39.50 guidance. Z39.50 Maintenance Agency (Congress Library) and its potential successor ISO Z39.50 are protocols that define data structure and allow bibliographic information to be searched or exchanged across distinct platforms in a distributed context.

5.1.4.1.6. Standards for Interoperability

Interoperability is the capacity to exchange information with minimum loss of content and functionality on various devices with distinct hardware or software platform, data structures and interfaces. Interoperability is therefore a key issue with a widening range of computer software applications, file formats, data and users in the networked setting. But in digital libraries and archives it is essential for digital preservation.

A. ODMA (Open Document Management API) : The Open Document Management API allows for inclusion in the ODMA compliant document management scheme of the proprietary implementation. Many packages of software for document management have already been complained about by ODMA.

B. DMA (Document Management Alliance) : DMA

is an integral standard for electronic document management (EDMS) interoperability. In order to fix the issue of data island that created distinct Document Management Software (DMS), for example, the Document Management Alliance attempts to MS-Word.

5.1.4.2. Advantages Of Digitization

1. Remote Access : Connect individuals worldwide through continuous free access online.

2. Multiple Accesses : Multiple access records are one of the main advantages of digitization. If a manuscript is physical, only one person may handle it over the period but several users may access that document simultaneously through the digitalization process.

3. Preservation and Conservation : Addressing environmental, ignorance, and destruction losses of heritage.

4. Dissemination and Promotion : It saves invaluable assets to enrich and illuminate the present. The online dissemination of information and culture is a phenomenon of the 21st century.

5.1.4.3. Barriers in Digitizing

1. At first nobody understood the digitalization, so everybody doubted in submitting his or her digital manuscript.
2. There is no doubt that 27 million documents from government, university and private records should be digitized at current.
3. At first, they sent requests for digitalization to the public but now the scenario has changed; the request is sent to the public.
4. It takes around 10 years to clear the pending applications.
5. Masses need to be made aware of the conservation of the archives so that this patrimony can be

transferred to the future generation.

6. A great deal of cash is needed for digitization. Therefore a fresh "adopt one book" digitization system has been launched.

CONCLUSION

Digital conservation will involve some sort of organizational conversion in all its dimensions. In today's era, long-term document conservation is a hot problem. In 20 or 100 years ' time, accessing digital records will be unavoidable if individuals do not process digital records as a bit stream. There are no fragile digital documents. Digital conservation is a significant problem for all due to the pace of technological obsolescence.

Nowadays, we recognize the canonical requirements for digital preservation, and the world's main libraries and archives focus on digital preservation and the born digital data for the future generation. As a result of ever-growing digital availability of materials, access and distribution are not only possible, but also a medium and long-term conservation of digital objects. But there's no static issue of digital conservation and technological advances will continue to develop.

5.2. CHALLENGES AND STRATEGIES FOR PRESERVING DIGITAL CONTENTS

Electronically, the conservation of records, e.g. digital preservation, was aided by information technology. The primary sources of data are important texts or records. In the organization and management of data, the system of information and communication technologies (ICT) has brought revolutionary changes. The information technology is currently offering the infinite chance to preserve non-digital records using the digital preservation facility. A suitable significance is now provided to the digital document conservation. The digital materials cover texts, databases, pictures still and moving, audio, graphics, software and websites, in a broad variety of ways. They are often short-lived and involve deliberate manufacturing, maintenance and management. Many of these resources have enduring value and importance and should therefore be safeguarded and maintained for present and future generations. Digital conservation is the process of keeping digital items accessible over time. As a crucial aspect of the modern setting, it has proved. Digital material relates to any computer-processed material and involves both digitizing and "born digital" resources. In this connection, long-term measures should be taken to cover the effects of altering technology for decades and centuries.

5.2.1. Digital Preservation

Digital conservation involves a number of measures to ensure continuous access to digital products as long as needed. For a certain period of time business requirements, as long as necessary could mean in the undefined future, or short term. According to the Encyclopedia of Information Technology, the term digital reservation is defined as the' process of keeping, under conditions that are adequate for its use, material produced in digital formats. It is defined in ALA (2007) as' digital preservation combines policies, strategies and measures that guarantee access to digital content over time. The uselessness of computer equipment, software and storage media compound physical conservation problems. Refers also to the exercise of digitization in non-digital format products such as printers, movies, etc., to avoid losses caused by the decay of the physical medium.

5.2.1.1. Two Types of Documents

Digital preservation concerns two types of documents namely born digital documents and digitally created documents. Born digital documents: This refers to those materials that were initially created using some form of digital technology. It is often referred to as electronic records. Documents that are digitally produced: this relates to products transformed by some reproductive means from analog to digital form, such as reception of data or scanning of text or items etc.

5.2.1.2. Objectives of Digitl Preservation

The main objective is to preserving and providing continued access to digital material, together born digital and digitized material, others are;

- To ensuring that preserved digital materials are authentic;
- To preserving damage and deterioration of the physical media by ensuring an environmental control;
- To reversing damage, if it's possible and
- To changing the format of digital materials to preserve their intellectual content, if it's necessary.

5.2.1.3. Principles of Digital Preservation

The fundamental principles of conservation used for the conservation of analog media also apply to digital conservation:

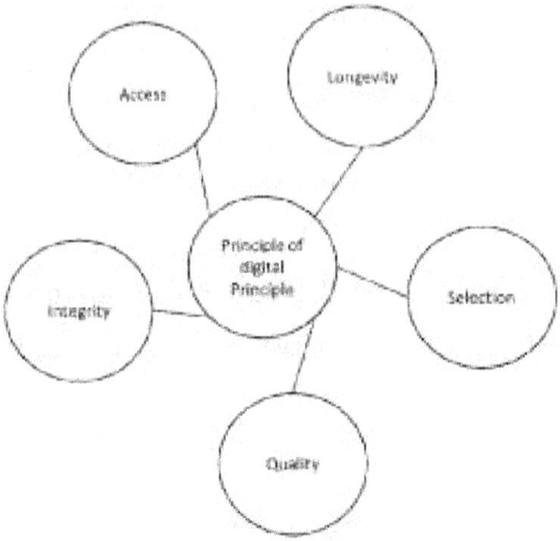

Fig. 1. Principles of DP

Longevity : the fragility of digital works makes information saved in digital format nonexistent. Replication adoptions and redundancies of the hardware, software and data formats mean that what can be read and understood today can be used for longer periods of time.

Selection : Multi-stage process selection is here. Every phase offers distinct methods to proceed. Selection of media and formats is either a choice of digital preservation products, or a range of instruments and technology. In the achievement of the conservation plan each choice plays a very significant part.

Quality : Digital content quality is needed in three phases. Firstly, during workflow specifies; secondly, when digital capture has been selected and handled; and thirdly, when the download time and user friendly formats have to be assessed during delivery and access time. The quality of digital documents is guaranteed by consistency.

Integrity : The access to digital content is protected by completeness, even if we remove the initial storage media, software and equipment that has produced, preserved and accessed digital content. The digital integrity of digital material also requires the development of methods for checking its initial format modification.

Access : Access to digital content is another important factor when we put in place precious internet access resources. The access to its digital content is a matter of policy for any library.

5.2.1.4. Dimensions of Digital Preservation

Digital preservation operations may generally be broken down in two parts:

1. Those which encourage digital image maintenance in the long term;
2. Those which make the contents of digital images continuously available.

Long : Term preservation: continuous access, or at least permanently access, to digital materials.

Medium : Term Preservation: Continued access to digital material for a specified time span but not permanently after technological modifications.

Short : Term Preservation: Access to digital materials is anticipated either for a fixed period during use but will not extend beyond the foreseeable future and/or until it is unavailable due to technological change.

5.2.1.5. Digital Preservation Challenges

For libraries and IT centers, it is a big challenge to tackle the transforming digital preservation technology. To recognize and assess their prospective effect, a thorough assessment of the risk variables connected with digital preserving should be done at an early point. Before digital preservation, the following are some significant difficulties.

Nature of digital materials : Technological changes mean that the timeframe for actions is much shorter than the timeframe for paper measures during which action is needed.

Dependency of Machine : Specific hardware and software are necessary to access all digital materials.

Fragility of the media : The digital materials are stored on is inherently unstable and without suitable storage conditions and management can deteriorate very quickly even though it may not appear to be damaged externally.

Shorter life span of digital media : The digital materials stored on are intrinsically volatile and can degrade very rapidly without adequate storage circumstances, even if externally damaged.

Formats and styles : There are significantly more impacts than on paper in allocating priorities. In future, it will probably be lost or unusable to choose a digital resource not soon chosen for active conservation therapy. The technology's nature needs the maintenance of a life-cycle strategy.

Copy rights and intellectual property rights (IPR) : The biggest challenge is not technology, but copyright problems, to make works accessible to the public in digital form. A digital library that makes its collection available on the internet is no longer just a place for collecting, preserving, and leasing something that others produce; it creates new exemplars with the same status as the digital original, because of its digital presentation. In a publisher there will be more or less like a digital library that makes its collections available over the Internet.

5.2.1.5. Preservation Strategies

In the digital conservation process, a wide variety of approaches are selected and implemented to attain the type of availability mentioned above and to address the conservation requirements of the distinct digital object layers.

- Setting the material secure location is part of the strategy.
- To recognize that trying to maintain everything is not practical, and to select which material should be maintained.
- Material control, structured metadata and other paperwork to make access easier and all conservation processes assist.
- Preservation of information integrity and identity.
- Choose suitable means in the face of technological change to ensure access.
- Administration in time, cost-effective, integral, proactive and responsible methods of conservation programs.

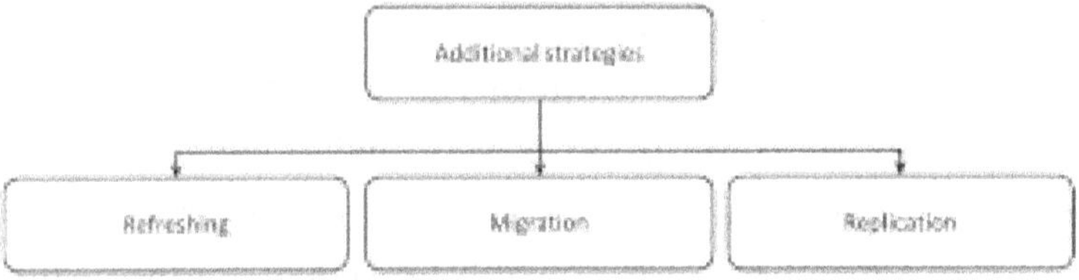

Fig. 2. Additional preservation Strategies

Refreshing : Refreshing is the transmission of information between two kinds of the same medium so that no change in bitrate or modification in information is possible. For instance, census data is transferred from an old preservation CD to a new one.

Migration : The transmission of information to newer system settings is migration (Garrett et al., 1996). The scheme involves the transformation of file-format resources from MM Word to PDF or Open-Document, Windows to Linux, or from one of its programming languages to another, for example, C to Java.

Replication : Emulation is a replica of outdated system functionalities. This involves the transformation of resources from one file format to another. For example, emulating a Windows system with Atari 2600 or emulating a Macintosh with WordPerfect 1.0. For apps, OS or hardware platforms emulators may be constructed.

5.2.2. Preservation Planning

The purpose of the Preservation Planning function is to monitor threats to accessibility, and to specify action to pre-empt or respond to them. The relevant threats mostly relate to changes in the technology that underlies access, so this function looks for such changes and takes action to maintain accessibility despite these changes. Frequently, the action will involve changing the information package: transforming the digital object itself to a different coding (as happens in migration), or changing the metadata that describes the means of access and links to current access tools.

5.2.2.1. Benefits of DP

- Ensure that accountability is strengthened.
- Plan consistent programs for digital conservation.
- Developing a plan for digital conservation.
- To show the use responsibly and consistently of such resources.
- To ensure the present and future use of digital materials available.
- Define the key characteristics for specific classes of resources that need to be maintained.
- Agencies to support the design of digital programs.
- Provide a full digital conservation declaration.
- Providing safety measures that guarantee digital materials are protected during use.

5.2.3. Digital Preservation Policy

The digital preservation policy could ensure a wide variety of organizational advantages, including ensuring present and future use of digital materials, giving an exhaustive explanation on the topic, and planning consistent digital preservation programmes. Further over, the policy formulation allows for difficult subjects such as the short-term life and small capacity of digital materials, the obsolescence of access hardware, the obsolescence of data and file format reader software, and lastly, the structural and technical heterogeneity of different types of digital materials.

Concept of Digital Preservation : Digital preservation is not a fresh idea; it started with the introduction of the first computers. In the late 1980s, several national libraries, national archives, data archives, and other institutions of culture in nations created their programs of digital preservation. These programs gave result with the current technology and digital content. Changes in potential capacities for both creating and preserving digital content in each technology generation and will result in an appropriate institutional response. Although technology is a key element in the digital preservation, we do not think it is the biggest inhibitor-despite increasing evidence that digital content is fragile and ubiquitous, the lack of organizing will and means has been slow in responding to the need to safeguard digital heritage.

Importance of Digital Preservation : A number of variables linked to library materials have contributed to the significance of digital conservation. A new era is emerging in the growth of digital resources in libraries of all kinds. Libraries always have historically concerned themselves with managing and preserving the' atoms' and today progressively need to concern themselves with preserving' parts.' The preservation of physical books and journals has its own issues, but domestic books and University libraries have centuries-old copies of books which, in many instances, have been kept untouched. But the large issue for libraries today is how library materials can be preserved.

5.1.4.1.1. Preservation of Digital Materials

Obviously, digital preservation is more than just data maintenance. The perspective of digital conservation that has been mentioned so far includes:

- Data preservation as a bit flow.
- Preservation of data (generally referred to as metadata) information.
- To ensure it is possible to find information.
- Ensures the retrieval and access of information are feasible and
- Provides a means to re-creator or re-present information utilization experiences.

Asking for managers to preserve data is to describe what knowledge needs to be replicated appears to lead us far beyond what the content of books or paper documents is expected to do. On the other hand, the best conservation programmes, in the method of non-digital materials, were probably similarly holistic.

5.2.1.5. Digital Preservation Challenges

It is difficult and complicated to preserve and especially digital preservation. No medium is immune to harm and decay when recording expressions of human creativity, thought, and achievement. In this respect, the long-term preservation of digital data is no different from the challenge faced for generations of cultural repositories. Yet digital preservation introduces its own distinctive challenge resulting from the fundamental nature of digital data-the digital preservation system is machine-readable, non-eye-readable and not as simple as the decoding method of the other machine-dependent media like micro-films or LP's. The technological obsolescence of hardware, software and formats into media vulnerability, conflicting interest of user's, organisational and legal problems and resource needs poses a major challenge for Digital Preservation. We can therefore say at the end that "digital conservation is an uncertainty zone in the pursuit of conservation alternatives with experimentation and discovery."

The Digital Preservation and Technology

- Identify important precedents, professional, organizational and technological milestones.
- Illustrate how we combine trends, activities and choices to where we are now in terms of digital conservation techniques.
- Helps in putting new and advanced technology in digital preservation programs context

5.2.3. Digital Preservation Policy

To ensure access to digital material, which are under

the care of Digital Repositories of University Libraries for an extended period determined by striking a balance between the needs of users and the priorities of the University Libraries, the preservation shall include all management and financial aspects. These operations include, but not restricted to, the provision of repository facilities, storage, policy development, and preservation of digital products and data.

Digital preservation policy of the University Libraries outlines a plan to promote sustainable access in the foreseeable future to the selection of digital collection content. The new and developing technology will change this approach, as digital content preservation impacts.

5.3.5. Education and Professional Development

In seeking and participating in training and professional development (CPD), library staff are very active and we organize awareness-raising and training sessions at any time and are trained to participate in professional conferences and co-workers conducting academic or accredited training programs. Team members also train each other in the essential skills for the use of systems or software and involve new staff. This all contributes to a wide range of CPD activities, which is why the library management team considered it appropriate to develop policy: in order to provide the employees with a strategic monitoring of the work of training and development, and to ensure equality in accessing these opportunities.

I am very happy that the driving force behind the creation of an employee development policy is a desire to develop. I am, however, aware that other people's experience in training and development involvement is quite the opposite, with ambivalence, lack of enthusiasm and institutional culture preventing proactive training and development. It is therefore useful to begin a personnel development policy by calling into question the need for

CPD.

5.3.8. Partnerships

Partnerships are highlighted in the eighth Millennium Development Goal as a strategy for development, and poverty alleviation. The capacity of information as a development tool is equally widely accepted and it is not surprising that the public libraries should be referred to as' natural partners' in community development as recognized providers of information services with information professionals. There is evidence that local libraries are expected to provide services that contribute to community development by the general public and other stakeholders. Research on African public library perceptions found that many people visit libraries to find information on issues such as health and the development of small businesses. The study also found that the majority of government officials and librarians believe Public libraries have a role in improving life in areas such as health, education, economic development and communication.

5.3.15. Library Associations

The contemporary is changing and increasing its scenario through the rapid development of latest technology. Library Association is the cornerstone by which the structure of library movement can be erected. It plays an important role in developing its library and library as a good profession. The first Library Association was founded in 1876 and the second was the Library Association of Great Britain. A country's library evolves according to its association of libraries. The Association of the Indian Library (ILA) was founded in Calcutta on the 22nd of September 1933. It is the largest and renovated professional library organization in the field of library and information science in India. There are other library associations in India, such as IASLIC, CGLA, IATLIS, MALA and DLA, which provide useful messages, guides to library developments, help to share opinions and promote free access to information and improve library activities. There are several other library associations in India as well.

Standards : Standards are policies which describe the values and performance of common academic library values for the bookstore of an institution in Carnegie. To be classified as standard, a document must have:

1. Objectives for programming, services and staffing in a library.
2. Serve the quantity, quality, extent and suitability as a rule or model.
3. Qualitative and/or quantitative support criteria, both undergoing further review.
4. Act as a criterion for decision making and actions in academia to confirm in relation to value, quality and adequacy the planning and management of library programs and services.
5. Suggest results in the areas described in the standard to be achieved by academic libraries.
6. Include statements related to performance related to reference population standards in related terms.

Guidelines : Guidelines are procedures which are useful when complying with the standards. To classify a document as a guideline, it must:

1. Be program-specific, service specific, or staff specific.
2. Identify the policy and procedural development framework.
3. Defines qualitative criteria; excludes quantitative criteria in general.
4. Identify factors that contribute to efficiency.
5. Build benchmarks that can be used to evaluate programs, services and staffing.

CONCLUSION

In the latest developments in ICT and the new potential to build a worldwide knowledge base, libraries and data resources centers have interesting possibilities. The challenge for both archive organizations and libraries is digital preservation. Commitment to digital conservation means a systematic project, which requires the existence of all the principles, policies and strategies that control activities to ensure the stabilization and safeguarding of intellectual content in physical and technological terms. This article outlined a methodology for extending current products and constructing new ones. While these offers are undergoing conversion, we are confident that our attempts to preserve digital technology were important to consumers in centuries to come.

5.3. ROLE OF INTERNATIONAL/NATIONAL ORGANIZATIONS

Library organizations are of major significance to bookstores, the profession and the community at domestic, regional and global level. This section gives a short summary of the role of library organizations and an overview of the organizing and difficulties faced by organizations. It involves an examination of the evolution of domestic, regional and global organizations, as well as examples of how domestic library organizations participate in global operations. It ends with a focus on the International Library Associations and Institutions Federation's worldwide operations.

In the 21st century, the worldwide community is a reality. Many of the domestic problems for library companies are now global problems, such as copyright and technology. Decisions taken at global locations can now dramatically influence how libraries can work and what services they can provide in a particular nation. Library organizations worldwide must therefore work together, share experiences and thoughts about projects beyond their boundaries. The new information age has allowed libraries to expand data and services supplied by the internet, digital collection and new techniques exponentially. Libraries and librarians must consider fresh technologies and services in adaptation and implementation. Libraries will not be on the fringes of the information age without enhancing facilities in order to meet user requirements.

As Narayanan Rakunathan aptly describes — "Library organizations offer librarians the chance to learn from each other and to share experiences. They provide a variety of facilities and care for employees. They function as the ideal point of contact for people interested in working with the industry. Although library associations serve their members ' needs, the end uses of services provided by these members are the long-term beneficiaries.

5.3.1. Roles

Library association gives the professional members the opportunity to work together to achieve the shared goals of professional, library and library service development. The roles of library associations are similar at a local, national or international level. Here are some of the main positions of library organizations that are closely linked.

5.3.2. Networking

Associations enable for interactions among professionals. All other functions of library organizations are the result of people gathering to share experiences, information and thoughts. Networking improves the performances of each person and offers an chance to share views and to work together for the better. Imagine how isolated a librarian is in the Pacific on a tiny Kiribati atoll. But it has the capacity to communicate with others across the area through meetings and training and through PIALA to the remainder of the bibliotheque industry, through the Pacific Island Association of Libraries and Archives (PIALA).

5.3.3. Leadership

Management is also what a library association brings beyond libraries to the profession and the world. Working together as a collective organization offers possibilities to enhance library and professional development. The National Library of Uganda Act of 2003, established and maintained by the Uganda National Library of Uganda and the creation of an information referral service, provided for the deposit and conservation of publications, provided for the management of the Uganda Library Association (ULA).

5.3.4. A Voice

Individually, recognition and objectives are very difficult to attain and almost impossible to influence society. Easily, one voice is gone, but an organization of hundreds or thousands offers a united voice representing everyone, a voice which is heard particularly by people outside the library community on problems such as the significance of literacy, the need for data policies and equal and fair access to data. The Australian Library and Information Association (ALIA) spoke in favor of establishing library employees in New South Wales as part of a focus group on pay equity assessment. This resulted in librarians being recognized for their professional status and pay rises.

5.3.5. Education and Professional Development

In this fast developing world, library organizations are a key to the further growth of the profession. Librarians must be trained to comprehend fresh thoughts, new techniques and new services and adapt to this. Associations provide possibilities for education by means of lectures, workshops, journals, etc. At its training center in Tbilisi, the Association of Information Specialists in the Republic of Georgia offers much needed information training to librarians. In the growth of educational norms for the profession, associations can also play an influence. It is in the United States and Canada the American Library Association that establishes the Guidelines and the accreditation of library schools.

5.3.6. Standards and Best Practices

The associations in the library draft and implement norms, rules, codes and best practices, etc., and thus enhance and enhance the profession. Many organizations have established ethics codes which form the basis of the profession, such as the Korean Library Association. In conjunction with the Canadian Library Association, the Australian Library and the Information association, the United Kingdom Charted Institute of Library and Information Professionals, and the American Library Association, the English-American Rules of Cataloging were adopted.

5.3.7. Advocacy

Library organizations operate to make libraries and librarians more visible to society, to promote public advocacy and to directly promote law making and fund libraries for legislators and policy-makers. The Armenian Library Association is, like many others, organizing a domestic library week, which gains domestic advertising and focuses on libraries. A "No al Prestamo de Pago" camp to combat the legislative efforts of authors and authors in order to receive fee charges through libraries and institutions through the use of public material. the FEDERÁTION Espanola de Sociedades de Archivistica Biblioteconomia Documentacion y Museística (FESABID)

5.3.8. Partnerships

Library associations build strategic relationships and partnerships with others interested in libraries, such as foundations, corporations, government entities, nongovernmental organizations, and schools. These partnerships can be valuable to associations, which usually do not have enough resources on their own to achieve some of their goals and objectives. For example, IFLA's Advancement of Librarianship Programme (ALP) has been supported with cooperation by the Nordic Library Association by funds provided by the Swedish International Development Cooperation Agency (SIDA).

5.3.9. Organization and Challenges

Similar organizational structures are being applied by library associations but members ' support, staffing and admissibility differ. The majority of the library organizations, however, have a powerful link to the state in some nations, such as China or Cuba. Even some autonomous library organizations, including the Danish Library Association, are eligible for direct public funding for particular operations.

The task of each association of libraries determines their membership. Some organizations are limited to librarians only. In others, the membership is comprised of organizations. Some membership organizations are purely individual, while some allow for private and institutional membership. Some people can also join outside of the industry, like the supplier group of the library, library followers and library employees.

Similar difficulties face library associations worldwide. Sustainability is paramount. Library organizations need human and economic resources to survive and flourish at all levels. Human capital is available in two types: employees and members. Unless members are actively involved in the Association, Library organizations are not powerful. Many organizations are too tiny to pay for the employees and therefore depend on their members' voluntary attempts to manage the association. Library organizations need to work hard in order to develop and sustain projects to hire fresh participants for sustainability.

Library organizations also need funding. Most library organizations depend mainly on their funds ' membership fees and conference income. These sources of income can often be minimal, particularly in the developing globe. Publications, trainings and grants are other feasible income areas for library organizations.

Despite these difficulties, library organizations, even without a workforce and very little cash, are very effective around the globe.

5.3.10. National Associations

The growth of domestic organizations in libraries has, as anticipated, more or less reflected the overall historical growth and change of nations all over the globe. In North America and in Europe at the end of the 9th century, the development of national library organizations started. The American Library Association was founded in 1876 by Melville Dewey, the creator of the Dewey Decimal System and others. It was the following year, in 1877, that the Library Association (United Kingdom), now called the CILIP, formed itself.

Library organizations started their training in nations throughout continental Europe, including association of librarians from Austria and librarians in Austria in 1896, the association of libraries and librarians from Switzerland in 1897, and the association of French librarians (ABS) in 1906. Many new national library associations have been reconstituted with the break-up of the Soviet Union. Originally established in 1931, in 1990 the Lithuanian Library Association was re-established and in 1995 the Russian Library Association was established.

Apart from these domestic organizations, in the United States and Europe, library associations were also established for special fields. Among these are 1896, the American Law Library Association; 1898, 1909, the

Association of the Medical Library; 1929, the Finnish Research Library Association.

Asia and the Pacific were the first domestic library association outside of the United States and Europe established in 1892 by the Japanese Library Association. In 1910, the New Zealand Library Association and in 1922, the Philippine Library Association were other early domestic associations in the area. In Latin America it took a little more time to create national library groups, the first being the Mexican Library Association, A.C. In 1924 (AMBAC), the region was not established until the 1950s or later by other national library organizations.

The South African Library Association, the first domestic library association in Africa, was established in 1930 and became an entirely white apartheid organization in 1962. The Association of South African Library Workers in Black Library was founded in 1964. The South African Library of Information Association (LIASA) was founded in 1997 by mergers of distinct organizations. In 1946 was founded what is now the Association for the Egyptian Library and Archives. The independence from the colonial rule began in the 1960s with national library organizations in other nations. Originally established as a Library Association of Rhodesia and Nyasaland in 1959, the Zimbabwe Library Association was established. Founded in 1962, the Nigerian Library Association.

Before independence was established the Indian Library Association, but only in 1967 was the Association founded. After 2000, national bookshop associations, such as the Uzbekistan Library Association, established in Eurasia. Library organizations in the Middle East started in the 1950s and' 60s, with the ILL in 1952, the ILL in 1960, the Iranian Library Association in 1966 and the Iraqi Library Association in 1968, respectively. The establishment in 2005 of the Association for the Kuwait Library has only begun with the development of national library organizations in the Gulf region.

5.3.11. Regional Associations

In order to work together librarians, libraries, bibliotheks and library organizations, many regional library associations have been created in relation to national library organizations. Some operate on a number of problems, while others offer networking possibilities in their area. The EBLIDA is an autonomous association of the domestic library, data, records and archive bodies and organizations in Europe. The EBLIDA is a domestic association of autonomous libraries and archive bodies. EBLIDA focuses on European issues of information society, including copyright, licensing, culture and education and expansion of the EU. They promote unimpeded access to data in the digital age and the role of archives and libraries to achieve this objective.

Groups like the Nordic Library Associations are meeting annually, by contrast, to discuss present issues, to keep each other informed about domestic trends and to work together on numerous advocacy and professional work. In Africa, the SCECSAL was established in 1957 by the Association of Eastern, Central and Southern African Libraries and Information Associations (EALA). The conference is organized biennially, offering networking and growth of professionals. Established in 1954, the West African Library Association (WALA) serves much as SCECSAL.

In 1970, in reaction to the increasing sense of Southeast Asian identity, the Congress of Southeast Asian Librarians (CONSAL) was established in Singapore, especially by establishing the Association of the Southeast Asian Nations (ASEAN). CONSAL represents 10 countries, holds a three-year conference and encourages cooperation in the areas of library, literary and documentation activities, as well as related activities.

Cooperation on the Caribbean and Pacific Islands is essential for regional organizations. An annual conference was held in 1969 and the Association of Caribbean University Institutional Research Libraries (ACURIL). In 1991, PIALA was established to organize libraries and archivists from seven different political areas in Micronesia. The PIALA island organization was established in the United States. An annual conference on various training problems is also held at PIALA.

5.3.12. International Activities of National and Regional Associations

These Library Associations are the fundamental backbone of global libraries, whether they are national or regional. They belong to IFLA and include individuals involved in global activities. There are certain global memberships for most domestic and regional organizations. The Special Library Association has members in 80 nations and chapters in areas throughout the globe, although it is mainly a US-based association. Associations like the Chinese Library Society and the ALA have time to encourage global work. Those who have no employees carry out their work through global boards. The government's or foundation grants support many global operations of national library organizations. National organizations can promote the exchange of librarians or visits from and to their nation. Some domestic associations have also been directly involved in supporting and providing help to other domestic associations. The Finish Library Association is involved in scholarships and training with the Library Associations of South Africa and Namibia (LIASA). ALA has given training for organizations in the Caucasus region with a grant from Carnegie Corporation. Membership dues of other nations are paid in IFLA by Associations in France, the Netherlands, Denmark and the United States.

National library organizations are also working to have representatives of different global delegations in their nations. For instance, in the Danish UNESCO National

Commission the Danish Library Association has an official voice. A representative at as many tables as possible is critically important for all national library organizations.

In crisis times, national organizations are also providing international aid. In the December 2005 tsunami ravaged Aceh Province, Indonesia, Persatuan Pustakawan Malaysia (Library Associate of Malaysia) was the principal contributor to the collectivity and support of libraries. The IFLA-sponsored training and workshops will be held in regional associative meetings. Regional associations are also used as a means of exchange.

5.3.13. International Associations

The Federation Internationale de Documentation (FID) was the first transnational organization established in 1895 for domestic documentation organizations. FID worked on the creation of the Universal Decimal Classification (UDC) which was first released in 1905. FID was responsible for the promotion "for studying and classification in general and for promoting a consistent scheme of classification in specific." More than 11 million entries rose in FID's Universal Bibliographic Repertory, a database. It also set up a global credit service, which was sent by e-mail and which received 1500 applications every year in 1912.

For much of its existence, FID had only seven members outside Europe at the end of 1958. FID dissolved owing to economic problems and ceased operations in 2001. Financial solvency is an issue in particular for international associations with great scope but often very small budgets and support from staff.

Many thought that the time had come to establish an global association of library organizations in the earliest 20th century with the proliferation and growth of domestic organizations. This led to the establishment in Edinburgh, Scotland, of the International Federation of Library Associations and Institutions (IFLA). Later in this section are discussed the creation and operations of IFLA. In 1948 the UN Educational Scientific and Cultural Organizations (ONUSCO) founded the International Council of Archives (ICA) for the establishment of a worldwide archive organization. ICA has a global network of more than 1.400 institutional employees, with present objectives in 190 nations: advocacy & advancement, automation and digital records, catastrophe prevention and conservation, as well as education and training. The project was developed "to enhance global norms of Archival and Practices and to promote archival theory."

A number of such international associations have been established in nations that mirror library-specific associations. A sample of these organizations is only available here.

- There are some 2,000 individual and institutional members in around 45 countries around the globe of the International Association of Archives and Documentation Cents of Music Libraries (IAML). Founded in 1951, it promotes international cooperation and fosters the profession's interests.
- Founded in 1959 and now with more than 600 employees across 5 continents, the International Legal Libraries Association (IALL) has over 50 nations. The participants comprise all kinds of legal collections, from libraries for scholarly law, corporate bookshops of all sizes, to domestic and parliamentary bookstores to public authorities, and court bookstores. The annual budget for IALL is approximately $100,000. In contrast to a conference focusing on a special area of legal libraries, it offers an annual course (for example, its "Legal Information in Multiple Legal System" was held in sites across the globe by 2008).
- Inaugurated in 1971, the International Association of School Libraries (IASL) provides an international

forum to promote efficient school library media as a viable tool of education. IASL offers advice and guidance to develop school library programs and professionals in the school library. IASL operates with other professional organizations and organizations in collaboration. 730 participants from 76 nations existed in 2008. The budget of the IASL is also very low of $50,000 per year.

International Associations and Institutions of Library Federation (IFLA) International founded in 1927, IFLA represents and customers of library and data services as the world-leading body. The goal of the IFLA is to: "Promoting high standards of supply, supplies or the provision of library and data services; Encourages a wider knowledge of the value of the excellent librarian & data services; represent the interests of all our members around the globe." In the 1950s, 41 IFLA members, including participants in China, India, Japan, Mexico and the Philippines, had been hired from 31 nations.

In Europe and North America, IFLA's first 45 meetings took place. A conference was held elsewhere only in 1980 in Manila. In Nairobi in 1984, the first IFLA Conference was held in Africa and was only held in Buenos Aires in Latin America in 2005.

Anyone who can attend the IFLA meeting can have an effect. In 2000 there were no librarians from other Middle Eastern nations attending the meeting in Jerusalem. In 1994, it was difficult for U.S. librarians to attend the conference in Havana and very difficult for Cuban librarians to attend in 2001, in Boston.

As the first, non-European / North American, to be elected President of IFLA, Kay Raseroka, Director of Library Services at the University of Botswana was made in 2003. By 2008, the membership of IFLA had grown to 1700 in 150 nations. IFLA has worldwide reach, but, as with many international organizations, it doesn't have a lot of funds. Indeed, the annual budget of IFLA is just around EUR 2 million and has only 11 employees. Only three peers, who supervise key operations such as the program of library growth and the generosity of the host organizations, will support headquarters employees. The official languages of the IFLA are Arabic, Chinese, English, German, French, Russian and Spanish.

IFLA is based in The Hague in the Netherlands Royal Library (which offers open room). It has a registered office. In various areas of the globe, three regional offices provide assistance. They belong to the Biblioteca Pública do Estado do Rio de Janeiro, Brazil, the Singapore National Library Board as well as to the University of South Africa. The IFLA's website is hosted in France by the Scientific and Technical Information Institute (INIST).

5.3.14. IFLA's Global Activities

IFLA embraced its three pillars, Society, Members and Professions at the end of 2004. The three pillars include: networking; management; a voice; training and growth; norms and best practice; advocacy; and alliances. They cover the main roles of library organizations.

The Society Pillar : In the past, IFLA concentrated a great deal on inner library operations. The internal improvement of the profession was the key activity of IFLA. However, it has now extended its task to reach people outside the trade.

Copyright and Other Legal Matters : Copyright and intellectual property matters once regarded the domain of countries are now global problems. International organizations [e.g. WTO and WIPO] are developing treaties and agreements which will have an effect on how libraries and library user's world wide access to data. The agreements and treaties will be drawn up by organizations in other countries.

In 1999, IFLA established a Committee on Copyright and other Legal matters with members from all over the globe to guarantee that library interests are represented. The IFLA subsequently requested the status of an observer to be able to send certified officials to WIPO, to WTO and ISO.

The IFLA controls and offers feedback by means of position documents and statements such as "The World Intellectual Property Organization's 2005 Library Related Principles for International Development Agenda" and "IFLA Digital Environment Copyright Position" (2000).

In order to ensure the frequent exchange of data, the IFLA developed excellent working ties with a multitude of other entities with comparable interests. The International Free Trade Organization (IFLA) has formal associate contacts with UNESCO and observer status with the United Nations. A number of non-governmental organizations, including the International Publishers Association (IPA), which has worked in cooperation with IFLA on joint statements in areas they agree on, have been given consultative status by IFLA.

Freedom of Access to Information and Freedom of Expression : In 1999, IFLA set up a Committee for Freedom of Access to Information and Freedom of Expression (FAIFE) to defend and promote the fundamental human rights defined in Article 19 of the "Universal Declaration of Human Rights" of the United Nations. IFLA promotes, through FAIFE in the field of libraries and library access, free access and free speech in all respects, whether directly or indirectly. FAIFE controls intellectual liberty in the library community throughout the world, promotes the creation of IFLA policies and collaboration with other global human rights organizations, and reacts to violations of liberty of access and speech.

FAIFE offers intellectual freedom training, particularly in connection with the IFLA's "Internet Manifesto (2002)," which encourages unimpeded Internet access by libraries and removes the obstacles to data flows that result in inequality. The World Report Series, which provides timely and comprehensive summaries of intellectual liberty and books globally, has been published by IFLA and FAIFE.

World Summit for the Information Society (WSIS): CLM and FAIFE activities provided the base for IFLA's participation at both the 2003 Geneva and the 2005 Tunisian UN World Summits for the Informing Society (WSIS). IFLA was involved in ensuring that the voice of libraries and society is represented in WSIS with the help of the Swiss Library Association. IFLA called for the promotion of libraries within the information society in the fields of information literacy and lifelong learning, electronic memory, global information common, equal access, and intellectual freedom under "Libraries @ the heart of information society." IFLA's attempts have acknowledged libraries as having a position in the WSIS Principles and action plan for the Information Society. IFLA is involved in follow-up conferences after the summits and has developed the Guidelines for International, Regional and Local Library Advocacy in relation to the application of the WSIS by the 2005–2015 action line.

International Committee of the Blue Shield : IFLA was one of the co-founding organizations of the International Blue Shield Committee (ICBS) following the massive destruction of cultural property at the beginning of the Iraq War, along with other international cultural organizations (e.g. the International Archive and International Museum Boards). ICBS shall act as a cultural Red Cross that protects cultural heritage by promoting the UN International Committee of Cultural Property Protection in the Event of Armed Conflict, formed in accordance with the Second Protocol to the 1954 Convention of The Hague.

5.3.15. The Professional Pillar

The professional pillar of IFLA focuses on IFLA's long-standing key operations to enhance professional practices and help libraries and data services support consumers in the quickly evolving worldwide setting.

Development of Libraries and Library Associations : IFLA is working to advance library profession, library organizations, library and data facilities in African, Asian and Oceanic developing nations and in Latin America and the Caribbean through its Action to Develop Library Program Associations (ALP). The Swedish International Development Agency (SIDA) is providing financing to ALP, which funds conferences, seminars, workshops, pilot projects and journals. By offering continuing education and training ALP supports new library associations and encourages information and communication technology (ICT) and digital resources development, supports librarians ' tasks (e.g. services to the public, data literature, lifelong learning and combating functional analphabetism). The IFLA is responsible for addressing the requirements and advocating interests of all kinds and sizes of library organizations through the Library Associations ' Management Section (MLAS). MLAS is committed to fostering and improving management abilities, sharing experiences and developing helpful seminars and workshops at the regional association development conferences in collaboration with ALP. MLAS oversees GLAD, a mentor-in-chief program intended to enhance Library Association Officers ' abilities and abilities in helping them run their associations. They are a mentor and mentor. MLAS has also developed guidelines on the development of policy and procedure, economic management, operation, public relations and more for library organizations.

Establishing Standards and Guidelines : The IFLA and the Conference of National Library Directors (CDNL) under the so-called "I FLA-CDNL Bibliographic Standards

Alliance" ICABL ensure that important actions for bibliographical and resource control of all kinds of assets as well as associated formats and protocol standards are continuously coordinated, communication and supported. In cooperation with UNESCO and the International Standards Organization (ISO), ICABS is working to achieve its objectives. The ICABS is aimed at maintaining, promoting and harmonizing current norms and advancing knowledge of questions linked to the long-term archival of electronic resources, including promoting new and suggested archiving conventions. Within the library and archives community, ICABS organizes workshops and seminars that will improve the communication on these problems. In 2003, IFLA created the Universal MARC (UCA) core activity to support the international exchange of bibliographic data, developing and supporting the Universal MARC format (UNIMARC). UNIMARC is now composed of 4 formats: bibliographical, authorities and holdings.

UNESCO also contracted IFLA to develop the' UNESCO Guidelines on the establishment of Digitization Programs in Libraries and Archives,' which are available to policy makers and executives in libraries and archives and in developing nations especially for digitization planning.

Preservation and Conservation : The primary objective of the preservation and conservation of the core activity (PAC) of IFLA is to preserve as much as possible in accessible form significant library and archive material, published and unpublished in all formats. The PAC, with the assistance of its regional centers, increases awareness of the basic place taken by the conservation of an organization in its leadership by experts and heritage experts, governments and the public.

It is through training staff and technicians that the PAC achieves this knowledge transfer, produced and disseminated information to raise awareness of preservation problems, evaluate needs through research, and promote national and international standards, guidelines and best practices in the field.

5.3.16. The Membership Pillar

The World Library and Information Congress : The IFLA should work together, like all library organizations, to make sure it remains dynamic, attractive and profitable and provides its members with necessary services. For the global library community, IFLA supplies a network car. The IFLA World Library and Information Congress (WLIC) takes place every August between 3000 and 5000 participants. Each one takes place in various towns all over the world. The delegates meet to discuss professional issues, to share experiences, to review and strategize new products and services.

5.4. INDIAN INITIATIVES TOWARDS DIGITAL PRESERVATION

This is a list of digital conservation projects to digitize current media or maintain current digital archives.

- ABS-CBN Film Restoration Project, an initiative to preserve the ABS-CBN Film Archives of tens of thousands of Philippine movies.
- The Archive Team records information on different websites and internet services.
- ARK maintains movie, video and audio media and photographs of species at risk.
- Canadiana.org provides non-commercial access to digital Canadian documentary heritage through an alliance of leading Canadian memory institutes.
- The Berlin Computer spiel Museum is cooperation partner of the PLANETS (Preservation and Long-Term Access through Networked Services) research project. In addition, it contributes to the Keeping Emulation Environments Portable EU Research

Project, a project that includes digital media preservation.

- The Digital Preservation Coalition (est. 2001) is a non-profit organization to safeguard digital sources.
- D-Space is open source program which mainly takes data in a variety of formats: text, video, audio or data, spreads the data over the web, indices the data and preserves the data over time.
- D-Space is open source software.

The Leibniz Information Center for Economics (https:/www.econstor.eu/dspace/about) The ECONSTOR is a non-profit electronic archiving service from the German National Economics Library. ECONSTOR seeks to maintain literature continuously in the economic and associated areas (http:/blog.repec.org/2011/09/15/econstor-a-repec-archive-for-research-from-Germany/). ECONSTOR also offers scientists in the fields of leadership, economics and social sciences a free open access publishing platform. Many editors now prefer to save ECONSTOR digital contents and archive them (http:/ijmess.com/whyijmess.php).

- Digital archive of Elsevier Science. In 2002, the Koninklijke library became the official digital archive of Elsevier science journals for seven terabytes.
- FP 7 (http:/durafile.eu), DURAFILE project. A novel software platform that protects both personal digital and digital information generated from organizations is designed for the DURAFILE Project (based on the FP7 Grant Agreement n ° FP7-SM-2013-605356 initiative). The International Dunhuang Project, an international cooperation to conserve, catalog and digitalize manuscripts, printed materials, paintings, textiles and artifacts on Dunhuang's eastern end of the SILK Route and other archaeological sites set up by the British Library, is an initial attempt to bring digital preservation to domestic users and

small and medium-sized enterprise

- LOCKSS, which was established in 1998 with the support of the Stanford University and is based on a distributed network of preservative appliances that runs the advantage of an advanced voting protocol, is developing and supporting digital open source software for preservation. LOCKSS is now used to maintain electronic theses and dissertation, public records, books, blogs, websites, collections of images and so on. It has been originally intended to maintain academic newspapers. The LOCKSS program operates its own network for conservation.
- National Digital Heritage Archives is a partner program for developing "Rosetta" digital archive and conservation management systems between the National Library of New Zealand, the Ex Library Group and Sun Microsystems. The program was introduced in early 2009 and was established in 2004.
- Meta Archive Cooperative is a collective, library-run digital preservation approach incorporating digital preservation infrastructure and knowledge in each of the Member Institutions that constitute the Cooperative. The Cooperative, which primarily includes the University library, acts as a network in which each retained file replicates seven times, is stored in geographical places throughout four nations and is managed closely from intake (as an SIP) to dissemination (as a DIP).
- The OPF is a non-profit member organization, supported by the technology and expertise for the long-term management of digital cultural heritage, which offers reliable alternatives for its employees to the problems of digital conservation.
- The OPF is an international non-profit organization.
- The US National Library of Congress, which was

established in 2000 with the aim of ensuring that information on digital, is available and accessible. Digital Information Infrastructure and Preservation Program.

- The Digital Archives in Pavia is a University of Pavia initiative promoted. It was founded in 2009 and seeks to gather digital indigenous archives and electronic records from members of today's culture and society, ensuring that they are conserved over time and study possibilities.
- Preserving the access to digital information (PADI) is an information file that was actively compiled and updated by the Australian National Library from 1996 through July 2010, which covers the topic of digital preservation. PANDORA, the Australian internet archive, still has archived variants of the PADI page accessible online.
- Rhizome's digital conservation program developing items such as Web recorder and Old web. Free open-source internet archiving instruments and the performance of heritage, digital cultural materials are available today.
- Portico, a non-profit organization that JSTOR initially launched in 2002 and provides a "permanent archive of electronic journals and books" for the digital preservation of the environment.
- RODA is the digital preservation open source repository which provides features for all major reference units of the OAIS model. RODA can access multiple kinds of digital material generated by big companies or public bodies in order to ingest, manage and manage them. RODA is based on open source technologies and supports the OAIS, METS, EAD, and PREMIS standard.
- The Shapell Manuscript Foundation is a non-profit US-based organization dedicated to preserving

historical records dating back to the 19th and 20th centuries with an emphasis on the history of the USA and the Holy Land. SMF has a wide range of digitized manuscripts on its website accessible for public viewing. SMF will also collect and digitalize a full list of Jewish troops that took part in the US civil war called the Shapell Roster Project.

- FDsys is a US Government Printing Office scheme created to authenticate, maintain and provide access to government-related data from all of the Federal government's three branches.
- Wiki Team, a group of volunteers with more than 4,500 wikis.
- The Digital Preservation Center of Excellence in Pune, India, is being created as a project flagship under the Ministry of Electronic and Information Technology's National Digital Preservation Program (NDPP), government of India in 2011. Several digital pilot repositories are under growth in various areas, such as government archives, e-government, culture and heritage. The NCAA is certified as a Trusted Digitals Repository under ISO 16363 on 27 November 2017. Among these are national cultural audiovisual archives.

CONCLUSION

The growth of libraries and the profession at local, national and international levels is critical for libraries organizations. They represent libraries, the profession and customers' needs, advocate and promote stances in problems that affect everyone, outside the library community. The importance of library organizations and the need to join and take part in them is crucial for people joining the profession. Library organizations will need fresh members to give energy and thoughts and to continue to succeed in future management.

REVIEW QUESTIONS

1. Explain digital preservation and its needs.
2. List out the challenges and strategies for preserving digital contents.
3. Explain the roles of International/National organizations?
4. Explain Indian Initiatives towards Digital Preservation.

References

- Alegbeleye, B. (2002). Preservation and conservation rationale, procedure, trends and benefits for research and scholarship being paper presented at the seminar organized by the National Library of Nigerian and UNESCO 4th – 5 th June, p 10 -11
- Alegbeleye, Bunmi. Disaster Control Planning in Libraries, Archives and Electronic Data Processing Centres in Africa. Ibadan: Options Book and Information Services, 1993.
- American council of Learned societies (ACLS) Newsletter 26 (1975): 1 -8
- American Institute for Conservation of Historic and Artistic Works. (2001). AIC Definition of Conservation Terminology. Washington D.C.: American Institute for Conservation of Historic and Artistic Works (AIC). 21-22.
- Ancient Scripts: Timelines. Retrieved on September 28, 2009 from http://www.ancientscripts.com/ws_timeline.html Ancient Scripts.com, 2008
- Anderson, H. and J. E. McIntyre. Planning Manual for Disaster Control in Scottish Libraries & Record Offices. Edinburgh: National Library of Scotland, 1985.
- Arora, J. (2004). Building Digital Libraries: an overview. Conference Proceeding of INFOGOLD. BIT, Mesra.
- Artim, N. 'An Introduction to Automatic Fire Sprinklers, Part I'. WAAC Newsletter, vol. 16 no. 3, September 1994.
- Artim, N. 'An Introduction to Automatic Fire Sprinklers, Part II'. WAAC Newsletter, vol 17 no. 2, May 1995.
- Artim, N. 'An Update on Micromist Fire Extinguishment Systems'. WAAC Newsletter, vol. 17 no. 3, September 1995.

- Artim, N. 'Cultural Heritage Fire Suppression Systems: Alternatives to Halon 1301'. WAAC Newsletter, vol. 15 no. 2, May 1993.
- Avedon, D. (1972). Microfilm Permanence and Archival Quality Standard. Special Libraries. 63, (12): 586-88.
- Avedon, John D. "Microforms as library fools" Library Trends 30 (1981): 253-265,
- Bailon, H. and Rather, J. (1955). Microfilm and Micro Fascimile Publications. Library Trends 4, (2): 182-94.
- Boone, M. D. "Monastery to marketplace: A paradigm shift." Library Hi Tech, 21.3 (2003): 358-366
- Brown, James W. A - V instruction materials and methods. New York, McGraw-Hill, 1959. p.116
- Browning, E. W. "More training needed in book binding and conservation". Library Journal .75(1950): 190-191
- Burkett, J. and Morgan, T.S., Eds (1963). Special Materials in the Library. London: Library Association.
- Carolyn, Arms R. "Historical collection for the National Digital Library". D-Lib magazine. (1997) Available from^Available from: http://www.dlib.org/armsc.html(Accessed on 23 January 2002)
- Carrying out a Library Security Survey and Drafting a Security Policy, 1992; How to Deal with Criminal and Anti-social Behaviour, 1994; Designing Out Crime, 1996. London: National Preservation Office.
- Chicago: American Library Association, Association for Library Collections & Technical Services, 1993.
- Clarkson, Christopher. "Conservation priories; A library conservator's view" In Conservation of library and Archives materials and the graphic arts. London, Butterworth, 1987 pp. 235-236
- Coilison, Robert L. "The treatment of special material in libraries". . London, Aslib, 1955: 77-86 73
- Collison, Robert L. Modern storage equipment and metliods for special materials in libraries Bath : cedric chivers, 1965 pp. 13-14
- Commission on Preservation and Access, Digitization as a means of preservation. 1997. Available from: http://www.clir.0rg/pubs/reports//digpres/digpres.html (Accessed on 23 January 2002)

- Conway, Paul. (1994). Digitizing Preservation. Library Journal. 12(1), 42-45.
- Conway, Paul. 'Archival Preservation: Definitions for Improving Education and Training'. Restaurator, vol. 10 no. 2, 1989.
- Cornell University Library (2003). "Digital Preservation and Technology Timeline". Digital Preservation Management. USA. Archived from the original on 6 August 2015. Retrieved 1 August 2015.
- Crawford, W. "Library space." Online, 23.2 (1999): 61-65
- Darling, Pamela W. and Wesley Boomgaarden, comps. Preservation Planning Program: An Assisted Self-Study Manual. Revised by Jan Merrill-Oldham and Jutta Reed-Scott. Washington, DC: Association of Research Libraries, 1993.
- Dempsey, L & Heery, R. (1998). Metadata: a current view of practice and issues. Journal of Documentation. 2 (54), 145-172.
- DePew, John N. A Library, Media, and Archival Preservation Handbook. Santa Barbara, CA: ABC-CLIO, 1991.
- Deutsche Bibliothek, Leipzig/Frankfurt am Main, 29–30 March, 1996. Amsterdam: European Commission on Preservation and Access, 1997.
- Digital Preservation, available at http://en.wikipedia.org/wiki/digital_preservation. accessed on 28 October, 2014.
- Disaster Preparedness: Guidelines for Archives and Libraries. London: Society of Archivists, 1996.
- Eden, P., & Matthews, G. (1996). Disaster management in libraries. LibraryManagement. 17(3), 5-12. Retrieved on January 5, 2015 http://www.emeraldinsight.com/doi/pdfplus/10.1108/01435129610112743
- Edward M. Corrado, Digital Preservation: The Next Library Frontier Presented at: IGeLU 2009, Helsinki, Finland, 8 September 2009
- Feather, John (1996). Preservation and the Management of Library Collections. 2nd Ed. London: Library Association Publishing.
- Feather, John and Sturges, Paul (2003). International encyclopedia of information and library science. 2nd ed. London. Routledge

- February 26-27, 2011,pp489-492.
- Fortson, J. 'Disaster Planning and Recovery: A How- To-Do-It Manual for Librarians and Archivists'. How-To-Do-It Manuals for Libraries, no. 21. New York:Neal-Schuman, 1992.
- Fothergill, Richard and Butchart, Ian (1990). Non-book Materials in Libraries. A Practical Guide. London: Clive Bingley.
- Fox, Lisa L., Don K. Thompson, and Joan ten Hoor (eds. and comp.) A Core Collection in Preservation.
- Fox, Lisa. L. 'Management Strategies for Disaster Preparedness'. The ALA Yearbook of Library and Information Services, vol. 14. Chicago: American Library Association, 1989.
- from: http://www.ala.org/ala/mgrps/divs/alcts/resources/preserv/defdigpres0408.pdf
- Gabriel, M. and Ladd, D. (1980). The Microform Revolution in Libraries. Greenwich, Connecticut: JAI Press.
- Ghani, Syed Raiyan. (2012). Digital Preservation: A paradox or sophism. SRELS Journal of Information Management. 49(5), 529-534.
- Giovannini, Andrea. De Tutela Librorum. Geneva: Les Editions Institut d'Etudes Sociales, 1995.
- Glosiene, A. "A Third Place." Presented at Information, Communication, Society International Conference, Tallinn University, Estonia, 8-10 October, 2005.
- Goel, Vindu (19 October 2014). "A Dynamic New Tool to Preserve the Friendsters of the Future". New York Times. Archived from the original on 23 April 2017. Retrieved 4 November 2016.
- Grimwood-Jones, Diana 'Preservation' In British Librarianship and information work 1981-85 Vol.2 Special libraries, material and process edited by David W. Broomley and Angela M. Allott London, Library Association, 1988 p.270
- Gunther, A. (1962). ,Microphotography in the Library UNESCO Bulletin for Libraries. 14, 1: 1-22.
- Hagg, D. (2002). XML and Digital Preservation. Retrieved from www.digitaleduc.zamhind.xl/does/xml.pdf
- Halder, Sambhu Nath. (2013). Library and Information Science in Changing Paradigm. Ess Publication: New Delhi,

207-215.

- Harrod, Leonard Montague. 'The Librarians' glossary. London ; clarion Books, 1977. p.657
- Harvey, Ross (1993). Preservation in Libraries: A Reader. London: Bowker.
- Harvey, Ross. (1994). Preservation in libraries: principles, strategies and practices for librarians. London : Bowker Saur.
- Harvey, Ross. Preservation in libraries : Principles, strategies, and practices for librarians. London, Bowker, 1993. p.6
- Hawken, W. (1966). Copying Methods Manual. Chicago: American Library Association.
- Hedstrom, M. (1997). Digital Preservation: A Time bomb for Digital Libraries. Computers and the Humanities. 31(3), 189-202.
- http://noalprestamodepago.org/World Encyclopedia of Library and Information Sciences, Third Edition, 1993, American Library Association, various country reports.
- http://www.ala.am/eng/index.asp
- http://www.nzdl.org/gsdlmod?e=d-00000-00—off-0hdl—00-0——0-10-0—0—0direct-10—4———0-1l—11-en-50—20-home—00-0-1-00-0-0-11-1-0utfZz-8-00-0-0-11-10-0utfZz-8-00&cl=CL1.4&d=HASH01fd2e8f1c305b10d9bf3a7b.12&gt=2
- IFLA Journal: Volume 18, No.3, 1992
- IFLA Membership Directory, 2002-2003
- Ikoja,-Odongo, J.R.., "Public library politics: the Uganda perspective" www.ifla.org/IV/ifla69/papers/171e-Ikoja-Odongo.pdf
- Information Literacy Skills for College Librarians in Digital Environment, NCILSCLDE-2011,
- Jackanicz, Donald. 'Theft at the National Archives: The Murphy Case, 1962–1975'. Library and Archival Security vol. 10 no. 2, 1990.
- Johnson, C. A. and Griffis, M. R. "A place where everybody knows your name? Investigating the relationship between public libraries and social capital." Canadian Journal of Information and Library Sciences, 33.3/4 (2009): 159-191.
- Library Trend: Summer, 1995.
- Lisa, William B. "Selecting rare books for physical

conservation. Guidelines for decision making". College and Research libraries. .46 (1985). 153-159/

- Lyall, J. (1995). Disaster planning for libraries and archives: understanding theessential issues. (National Library of Australia Staff Papers, 1995). Retrieved onJanuary 5, 2015 from http://www.nla.gov.au/openpublish/index.php/nlasp/article/view/979/1249
- Lynch, Clifford. (1994). The integrity of Digital Information: Mechanics and definitional Issues. Journal of the American Society for Information science. 45. 737-744.
- Marray, J.A.YH. (et. Al.) Ed. The oxford English Dictionary Vol.6. Oxford, Oxford University press, 1978 p. 145
- Matick, R. (1977). Computer Storage Systems and Technology. New York: Wiley.
- Mazikana, Peter C. "A strategy for preservation of audiovisual materials" Audiovisual Librarian 14 (1988): 24-28.
- Modh, S. (2010). Introduction to disaster management. New Delhi: MacmillanPublishers India. p.18
- Moon, Myra Jo. 'Reducing Theft, Mutilation and Defacement of Library Materials'. Conservation Administration News no.17, April 1984.
- Mosher, Paul H. "Manuscripts" In The worid Book Encyclopaedia vol.13 Chicago, World Book Inc, 1988 p. 172 Harrod, Op. Cit.
- Non-print media library management. Commonwealth Education Media Centre for Asia (CEMCA) workshop handout. New Delhi, 1997
- Pandher, Balbir kaur. (2012). Conservation and Preservation of Archives: A case study of Punjab Digital Library. World Digital Libraries. 5 (1), 75-84.
- Parker, E. (1985). The Library of Congress Non-print Optical Disk Hilot Programme. Information Technology in Libraries 4, 4.: 289-92.
- Pooja Sharma, Digital Preservation Technologies, Proceedings of the National Conference on
- Preservation (library and archival science) available at: *http://en.wikipedia.org/wiki/Preservation_(library_and_archival_science)*
- Priyolkar, A. K. 'Durmil granth Kashas Mhanave' Dnvangangotri 1 (2000): 1-10.

- Rakunathan, Narayanan, "Library Associations," www.ifla.org/VII/s40/pub/rakunathan.pdf
- Resource Conservation Alliance. (2008). Focus On Paper Consumption. Washington, D.C.: Resource Conservation Alliance.
- Retrieved from: http://pandora.nla.gov.au/index.html
- Retrieved from: http://www.digitalpreservationeurope.eu/
- Retrieved from: http://www.fedora.info/presentations/DLF-Nov2003.ppt
- Retrieved from: http://www.inflibnet.ac.in/caliber2009/CaliberPDF/11pdf
- Retrieved from: *http://www.interpares.org/ip2/ip2_terminology_db.cfm*
- Retrieved from: http://www.oclc.org/digitalpreservation/
- Retrieved from: http://www.oclc.org/research/publications/archive/2000/lavoie/
- Retrieved from: http://www.researchinformation.info/rispring03data.html
- Retrieved from: www.ncaonline.org.uk
- Rose, Frank (23 October 2016). "The Mission to Save Vanishing Internet Art". New York Times. Archived from the original on 25 October 2016. Retrieved 4 November 2016.
- Russell, Kelly. (1998). Skills requirements of LIS professionals in the new e-world. Library science with a slant to documentation.36, 141-149. Retrieved from http://www.ariadne.ac.uk/issue18/cedars/
- Saffady, W. (1985). Micrographics. 2nd Ed. Littleton: Libraries Unlimited.
- Schenck, T. (1984). Magnetic Tape Care, Storage and Error Recovery. Library Hi Tech 2, 4:51-54.
- Sitts, Maxine K. A Practical Guide to Preservation in School and Public Libraries. Syracuse, NY: Syracuse University, ERIC Clearinghouse on Information Resources, 1990.
- Skepastianu, M. and J. I. Whiffin. Library Disaster Planning. The Hague: IFLA HQ, 1995.
- Smith, J. E. (1881). A History Of Paper. Dalton: Paper World Press.
- Stevens, R. (1971). The Microform Revolution. Library Trends 19(2), 370-95.

- Stevens, R. (1988). Optical Disks Vs. Micrographics as Document Storage and Retrieval Technologies. Westport: Meckler.
- Stevenson, Condict Gaye. Working Together: Case Studies in Cooperative Preservation. Washington, DC: Commission on Preservation and Access, 1991.
- Storey, Richard, A. M. Wherry, and J. F. Wilson. 'Three Views on Security'. Journal of the Society of Archivists 10, July 1989.
- T. Kaur (2009). Disaster planning in university libraries in India: a neglected area.New Library World. 110(3/4), 175-187.
- Tanwar, Sundar Singh. (2012). Digital preservation. PEARL-A Journal of Library and Information Science. 6(2), 83-88.
- Teague, SJ. (1985). Microforms, Video and Electronic Media Librarianship. London: Butterworths.
- Teece, Phil, "Raising Library Salaries in New South Wales, Australia," www.ifla.org/IV/ifla71/papers/180e-Nicholson.pdf
- Trinkaus-Randall, Gregor. 'Preserving Special Collections Through Internal Security'. College and Research Libraries News 50, July 1989.
- Trinkley, Michael. Can You Stand the Heat? A Fire Safety Primer for Libraries, Archives and Museums. Atlanta, GA: Southeastern Library Network, 1993.
- Trinkley, Michael. Hurricane! Are You Ready for the Big One? A Primer for Libraries, Museums, and Archives. Columbia, SA: Chicora Foundation, 1993.
- Veaner, A. (1982). Practical Microform Materials for Libraries: Silver, Diazo, Vesicular. Library Resources and Technical Services 26(4), 306-308.
- Verry, H. (1952). Micro-opaques. Aslib Proceedings. 4, 3: 153-62.
- Weber & Dorr, M. (1997). Digitization as a method of preservation? Amsterdam: European Commission on Preservation and Access.
- Weihs, Jean, (et al). Non-book Materials, The Organisation of Integrated Collection. 2nd. Ed. Canadian Library Association.
- Wit; J. R. 'conservation' In The world book encyclopaedia

vol.3 Illinois : field enterprise educational corporation, 1959. pp. 1687-1692

- Wittich, Walter and Schuller, Charies francis. Audio-Visual Materials: Their nature and use. New York;, Harper & Brothers, 1953. pp.92-93
- World Encyclopedia, FID article
- World Encyclopedia, various country and association reports
- www.acuril.uprrp.edu
- www.consal.org
- www.eblida.org
- www.iall.org
- www.iaml.info
- www.iasl-online.org
- www.ica.org
- www.ifla.org
- www.ifla.org
- www.mangilao.uog.edu
- www.nla-ng.org
- www.scecsal.org